BOOKS BY JEFFREY THOMSON

POETRY

The Halo Brace

The Country of Lost Sons

Renovation

Birdwatching in Wartime

The Belfast Notebooks: Poems and Prose

MEMOIR

fragile

TRANSLATION

The Poems of Catullus: An Annotated Translation

ANTHOLOGY

From the Fishouse: An Anthology of Poems That Sing, Rhyme, Resound,
Syncopate, Alliterate, and Just Plain Sound Great

HALF/LIFE: NEW & SELECTED POEMS

JEFFREY THOMSON

HAL
/L

ALICE JAMES BOOKS
Farmington, Maine
alicejamesbooks.org

FIFE

NEW & SELECTED POEMS

10 9 8 7 6 5 4 3 2 1

Alice James Books are published by Alice James Poetry Cooperative, Inc., an affiliate
of the University of Maine at Farmington.

Alice James Books
114 Prescott Street
Farmington, ME 04938
www.alicejamesbooks.org

Library of Congress Cataloging-in-Publication Data

Names: Thomson, Jeffrey, author.
Title: Half/life : new & selected poems / Jeffrey Thomson.
Description: Farmington, Maine : Alice James Books, 2019
  Description based on print version record and CIP data provided by publisher;
  resource not viewed.
Identifiers: LCCN 2019012542 (print) | LCCN 2019015656 (ebook)
  ISBN 9781948579605 (eBook) | ISBN 9781948579049 (pbk. : alk. paper)
Classification: LCC PS3570.H6466 (ebook) | LCC PS3570.H6466 A6 2019 (print)
  DDC 811/.54--dc23
LC record available at https://lccn.loc.gov/2019012542

Alice James Books gratefully acknowledges support from individual donors, private
foundations, the University of Maine at Farmington, the National Endowment for
the Arts, and the Amazon Literary Partnership.

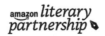

Cover art: John Tuomisto-Bell, "Falling Man #11", 2014, acrylic, pencil, charcoal,
rubber cement, sawdust, and gunpowder on canvas, 6'x4'

CONTENTS

This one is for all of you—
I hope you know why

We hope we remember all the words

—ELLA FITZGERALD

WHY I WRITE

I write to live my life in the open. I write to hide in plain sight.

I write because I want to understand what I think. I write because I don't know what to say.

I write to talk to myself.

I write to describe, to define, to tell. To tell on. To tattle to the world.

I write to impress women. And men.

I write because childhood is the country we all come from and to which we can never return.

I write to tell the story of the time I went up and up into the clouds of *Cerro de la Muerte*, riding my mountain bike for hours and hours again, all uphill, and the trees were drizzled with fog and moss and bromeliads, and my mind broke and I wept.

I write because desire.

I write to tell the truth. I write because I like to lie.

I write to talk about the feel of the rain on my face in the wind fresh off the Atlantic, the rough and marled coastline of Maine, black-backed gulls.

I write because when Ella Fitzgerald sang "Mack the Knife" in Berlin in 1960 she forgot the words and mangled the song just perfectly—her voice silk's idea of silk—as the rain smacked the streets outside the *Deutschlandhalle*.

I write because it is my job.

I write because I am not smart enough to do anything else.

I write because history: The Prague Spring, the first King of Ireland, or the time The Rolling Stones visited Tangier and wandered the Kasbah with *kif* and hash and those silver necklaces and strolled to the Café HaHa while the band was falling apart and Brian Jones was running towards his death.

I write because science and math.

I write because I cannot not.

I write because hummingbirds, and the bright, tiny flags of their bodies spangled in the sunlight beneath the heliconia, and their incomprehensible hearts. I write because quetzals, with their emerald tail feathers and crimson breasts. Because ospreys.

I write because it is what I love. I write because I hate it and want to be done so I can walk down to the bar and drink a beer and just watch the damn ballgame.

I write because I read.

I write to stop reading.

I write to describe the flight of pelicans above the Intracoastal Waterway and the old gray pilings and the light and the water thin and blue in the flats where the tarpon shoal.

I write because of my wife's breasts. And the breasts of other women. And the arms of men, muscled and tight, and their hips. Maybe I've said that already.

I write to describe the way the light lies down on the grass at dusk when I am sitting on my porch—it lies down like a blanket of gold, by the way—and the way my wine tastes and the air.

I write because of rain and silence. Silence and rain.

I write because I love the sound of words and the sense of sentences. I write because neither of these things are enough, because the words get it wrong and sentences are loose nets with which I try to haul up the sea.

I write to talk about the time I took a boat out onto the Gulf of Genoa and the sky was blue gauze and the dove-colored hills rose up beyond like distant history. I dove into the water and floated there, caught between the sky and sea. I write to understand how the world felt then: elegant and wet with promise.

I write because fallen angels fell in love with the daughters of men and taught them many secrets.

I write because for their sins they (and we) were punished.

I write to remember. I write so I don't forget. But I forget why, sometimes.

I write to tell the story of the time my heart came close to stopping and I had to kneel down in the middle of the street in Quepos on the tarmac hot and sticky and the sky was steaming blue and the bougainvillea flowed in purple waves over the walls of the houses and the dark crept in around my eyes. I write to get past that moment.

I write because I survived. But that's another story.

I write to talk about Achilles, and Plato, and John Keats. I write to have a conversation with Elizabeth Bishop. And Norman Maclean. And Larry Levis. And Penelope. And Terrance Hayes.

Oh, and God.

I write because I don't think God exists. I write to replace Her.

I write so I can talk to my friends—who are also writers—about what I have written and when.

I write to talk about the murals in Belfast, Northern Ireland, how in one the barrel of the machine gun of the man in the balaclava follows me like an eye as I cross the Shankill Field—that orchard of ruin with a no-man's-land inside it.

I write because Paris, because Rome.

I write because Maine and Iowa. St. Louis, too, lost in the gauzy wasteland of memory.

I write because people ask me to, sometimes.

I write whether I am asked to or not.

I write because there is a nameless beach in Corcovado where the water purls in perfect clarity on the olive sand and the sea turtles haul themselves out of the ocean to bury their eggs in pits they dig with their winged, inarticulate hands.

I write because those eggs glow like dirty pearls in the dark.

I write to avoid reading my email. I read my email to avoid writing.

I write because Cadmus was supposed to sow dragon's teeth and fight the warriors who grew from them, but being clever he tossed a rock among them and they turned on themselves in self-slaughter. I write because Cadmus was meant to marry the daughter of love and war, and the last time the gods sat down for a meal with men was at this marriage. The gods gave the couple many gifts that night, but the last gift they gave was the alphabet.

I write because all the stories told that night were new in a way they never could be again.

I write because my son will one day grow up and leave home and I will need to remember how he looked today, with the shock of his blond hair and his ferocity and his sadness.

I write because there is so much to tell him. So much.

I write because Orpheus in his grief sang to the trees and they bent their branches down to him.

I write because Eurydice returned to Hades.

I write because maybe, just maybe, it's the heartbreak of the broken, the simple wrongness of things that makes everything whole.

I write because my written life is the only life I truly own.

NEW POEMS

(2019)

SELF-PORTRAIT AS ISHMAEL'S ARM

— Scott Kelley, watercolor on paper

I am not what you are thinking.
I am the hitchhiker attached
to my own story. The long-
shoreman of history. I am
corpus and metaphysic.
I am whalebone and tendon.
I am *palmaris longus* and
the *flexor carpi*. I am speckle
and I am tooth. I am hunger.
I am Inuit and infinity. I am
the hand of God reaching out
to touch Adam, my billowing
Majesty, the brain-shaped cloud
I ride blustered with cherubim.
I am spine and I am snake.
I am the ship disappearing below
the horizon. I am the thin trail
of the railroad riding itself
across the country and vanishing
at the wrist of the river
where black firs crowd
the bank and water spumes.
I am riding the whale of my own
story into the future.

WHERE DO YOUR POEMS COME FROM?

In the Namib, fat sand rats saunter through
all the continents of their own personal deserts

I started this poem thinking about Orpheus,
because I am always thinking about
Orpheus, strumming as the dead stir

all the while, looking for death's hawk-shaped smear,
looking for amaranth seeds, small as the ball bearings

in the black thickets of Hades, the weeping
King and only the Queen dry-eyed.
This poem began for me as I thought

of the plane that taxis off the dirt track
runway and yanks itself into the sky

of my grandfather waking me to go fishing
in the early dark, even though
he never speaks to me as he opens up

meter by meter, the uneven slosh of the petrol tanks
in the wing and the sway of the plane

the door of this stanza and stands
in a sharp wedge of light. When
I was growing up, a friend and I traveled

in the wind, as the pilot follows the spikes
and hoops of vertebrae speckling the dunes

miles to sneak into an abandoned sand factory,
the catwalks and vats, the webbing of the windows
in the late light. So now when I begin

with the bray of the surf as it punts into the shore,
kicked there by a wind that began in

this poem talking about the lonely
architecture of memory, you know that
that is what I mean. I spent an afternoon in

Porto Seguro as the six-hour breath of the Amazon
huffed into the sea and the bore tides rode

Riomaggiore and watched cats come down
from the crumble of houses chasing each other
into the Gulf of Genoa. They came down

their stampede back into the trees, into the dim dim
forever dim twilight of the forest in the Tahuayo

as the fishing boats returned late in the day,
gathered around the beached hulls, and
waited for the heads and spare bait, waited

where hyacinth macaws gnaw at hillsides
of clay and nest in the great almonds

for the gift of a glassy eye. Late that night,
returning quite drunk from a café up
the coast, my boat pulled into the city

in a ruckus as a blessing of rain muscles
through the trees in the heat of the day, and

with only a few lights speckled up the sides
of the dark hills. The bakers were at work
and the town smelled of bread and yeast and

beneath the awning in sudden silence as the rain finishes,
I write in a book blanked by the last of the setting sun

warmth rising to the thin spackle of stars—
that's where this poem comes from—I bought
hot bread and tore it apart in the dark.

THE COUNTRY OF NOSTALGIA

If childhood is the country we all come from,

> *From the Greek roots*

flat brown ropes of rivers knotting continents

> *nostos (returning home) and*

to the sea, trees I scurried in a wash

> *algos (pain or longing).*

of summer wind, if the nights I spent

> *With the success*

tented beneath my sheets with a flashlight

> *of the neologism*

say something about what it meant to be a boy

> *people forgot*

compelled by books, if the time I passed

> *the origin of the word:*

in hiding, harbored from the searchlights

> *a medical condition*

of squad cars or fathers jabbing into every room

> *in which "the pain*

with their anger and an old bat, if the time I dropped

> *a sick person feels*

white crosses with Olshansky and ran miles

> *because he wishes*

to the Dairy Queen counts for more than decadence,

> *to return to*

it means I can never go home; although there are

> *his native land,*

lands where everyone's from somewhere else

          and fears never to see it

and they speak my name even as I tie up

          again" can be fatal.

to the dock, islands green as wine bottles

          (Johannes Hofer, 1688).

where I can drop my hand into the valley

          By the 1800s, it lost

between your legs and we can work together,

          the status of a disease;

like the old gods, to make the new earth bloom. I say,

          although cases

whatever heaven there is I lived there, navigating

          occasionally resulted

those summer nights when the air thrilled

          in death and as late as

with pollen and dust and the heat beat wings

          the Civil War

above my bed and I read until my mother woke

          soldiers were treated

and untied the light from my hand and pushed me

          by being sent home.

into the deep water of sleep.

ASBEEL

In the Book of Enoch, *God cast many angels out of heaven. Asbeel, the first,*
married a human woman and taught her the secrets of the natural universe.

Doppler Effect: In a blue dress, she walks through the burnt orchard,
dust rising in small scallops against her feet. The call of an owl
fills her mouth. Its sound clutters against my chest as I approach.
Her dress shifts to red as she moves away.

Uncertainty Principle: Distrust I can taste (Sancerre from a plastic cup,
silk flowers in cut glass, yellow jackets honeying nectar from an
apple core, the position of her tongue and its motion) when I
kiss her.

Mass-Energy Equivalence: The purple mouths of irises, pollen, the wings
of dead petals spread across the pages of a poem on the table.
Lines written in heaven and delivered here on earth.

The First Law of Thermodynamics: The heat from her hand on my chest
equals the heat from my chest to her hand. The fervor of me
entering her equals the radiance of her enveloping me.

Wave-Particle Duality: The owl call becomes an owl spinning its head in
the burnt orchard frosted with the green of new grass, a yellow
jacket sputters beneath a plastic glass, now empty, her wine-wet
lips. The poem becomes real as it is read aloud.

The Strong Anthropic Principle: We are with each other because if we weren't we wouldn't be able to consider being alone.

The Second Law of Thermodynamics: I burnt the orchard with the flame I am made of. I flung the owl into the dark knees of the distant trees. The flowers arrived out of the black soil and just as quickly returned. I finished the wine myself.

Occam's Razor: The possibility of her arriving in the orchard just as the flames died. The possibility of an owl hunting in daylight. The possibility of the wine. The possibility I imagined her from the start.

ADAM & EVE

Somewhere in between
I want to feel you inside me
and *Why won't you just
fuck me?*

                    stands a man in a spring field
                    green as silence, green
                    as an apple, green as rain.

      You might say the field
      is *desire*, you might say
      the field is *restraint*.

You might ask why
he doesn't take the apple
in his teeth and leave

            a small fence indented
            in its white earth.

     You might ask why
     and still not understand

                the swell of wind
                off the river, the belly
                of it hitting him

with an ache like sickness
and the fear he will never
make it home,
                  or you may have come
                  to hate him now

                    (as I have)   for all
                                      that he means and doesn't

say   and you may hate
                         the field and all
                         she asks of him in it

knowing what comes next   (as you do)
                                      is never enough.
                                      They still have to walk
                                      through those tiny gates.

SELECTED PERIODIC TABLE OF THE ELEMENTS (WITH NOTES)

Hydrogen (1)

    elemental

Helium (4)

    my throat tightened then

Carbon (12)

    damage that remains from a small scratch of fire on the ground

Nitrogen (14)

    azote, as Lavoisier calls it, *without life;* outside his window clover
    fields sway violet

Oxygen (16)

    without it, almost all known organisms die within minutes; too
    much, however, is toxic, like knowledge

Neon (20)

    after the radiography, I tried to drink the taste from my mouth
    beneath beer signs blanked in angled, afternoon sunlight

Aluminum (27)

summer nights—July's misery dying down, the Cardinals on the radio—the snap of the bat and its echo, the opening crack of a can of beer

Sulfur (32)

the smell of the canal, blue fescue, and the Florida sun—my grandfather, shirtless and tan on the dock, bones the trout we've caught, his quick wrists and the thin sharp knife

Calcium (40)

the cartoon flashes on the silver-threaded screen, clacking into the spokes of the empty reel and in the dark we watch milk slide down the cut-away throat of the boy, the gulped whiteness spreads through his chest to his bones

Titanium (48)

Challenger burst into a spider fern of smoke above the Cape that day and I watched on CNN then went to class where the professor said we could leave if we wanted to—if anyone was too affected by that flowering loss to continue—and no one did

Iron (56)

we were pitching nickels behind the cafeteria, the greased green bulk of the dumpster hiding us from the playground monitors, when I called big Sean Phillips a cheat, when he hit me; I stayed down as he swayed above

he was cheating, but I was the one on the ground tasting the metal in my blood

Copper (64)

the nine-volt flavor of wire as I split them and stripped their sheaths with my teeth—red to red, black to black—the small speakers, the turntable (outside the wind flustering the ratty trees) and Bob Marley's *Catch a Fire* crackles into the one room of my first apartment (small and greasy and over-painted) where I'm a little high in my castle of boxes

Selenium (79)

the moon gives no light of its own, though I can see by it the twisted path through the birches to the river crosshatched with shadow, the silver spangle of water moving over the collection of stones below the power plant, see the shadows of form and the smoke kicked out from the row of black stacks silhouetted in the summer night,

see the dark body of the world reflected in that light—toxic and necessary in equal measure

Krypton (84)

hard to see the story ending well when Marlon Brando, bloated and wet-lipped, places his son in the space craft (that future so gauzy, bright and clean) and of course the planet explodes, seeding itself across the universe, but this small boy is Moses for the atomic age and he is discovered in a Midwest sea of reeds plowed by the smoking ship

well-fed and invulnerable, he discovers that the only things that can kill him now are the fragments of his former life

Barium (137)

I sipped and swallowed on command, the mint flavoring added to the drink barely covering the taste of concrete and lime, then the machine's giant mind hummed and whirred about me, the cold vibrating up from the floor beneath the ludicrous gown (I've kept my socks on and my wallet's on the shelf)

day had dawned flat and gray with a white sun pasted across the horizon—I was awake too early—light swelling in the sky above the dark firs, no birds, and wind-drifted snow sluiced across the hospital's asphalt

I swallowed and swallowed and the radiation flashed through my chest and throat looking for the mass (that body within the body) they thought was there—the white bulk that glinted inside me—as the lead-heavy doctor and the two technicians watched, watched and said nothing

Promethium (145)

from clay he molds a single shape so carefully, this one body he loves even before he has finished it—all the while his brother bakes thousands and tosses them behind him, bewildered and feathered or clawed with damp fur—that when he is finished there is nothing left (the speckled scales and gills, the spotted pelt, the venom, all gone) and this delay leaves his creation alone and shivering in the cold so he conspires to steal fire from the chariot of the sun and carries it to earth cupped in leaves of fennel his punishment is well known—that body that grows and grows inside him, the daily growth and the pain—but when Herakles is done, the eagle skewered, and Prometheus is allowed again to join the crowd upon Olympus, he must carry with him the rock that he was chained to

Radium (226)

was used in self-luminous paints for watches, nuclear panels, aircraft switches, clocks, instrument dials, and in fact, the Radium Girls, more than 100 former watch dial painters who took brushes to their mouths to shape the tips as they stroked each watch face's tiny hands, died—

this doesn't mean anything, all my tests were negative, the half/ life of my life spins onward—

because they ingested the paint, took the decay products (once known as radium A, B, and C, but it is now known that the disintegration of the nucleus produces other atoms, other isotopes, other fragments)

into their mouths, the wet tongues of the brushes, the taste of metal—

this doesn't mean anything—

the women's faces glowed with the small light of their brushes, the workroom kept dim so their work would show, summer sunlight creeping in from beyond the blackout shades

this doesn't mean anything, the fragments, the pieces are only half the story they occasionally painted their nails and teeth and faces

a rock (an alkaline earth metal) that casts its own light—that's
all the metaphors for writing

this rock

this does not mean anything

the tiny whiteness spread through their mouth to their bones,
this flowering, this alphabet of probability

this rock I am

the tests were negative

they died

that does not mean anything

this rock I am chained to

BLINK—A SONNET FOR ANTOINE LAVOISIER, 1743–94

Condemned to the guillotine, Lavoisier told his assistant that, as a final experiment, he would blink as many times as he could once his head had left his body.

1. When my head first rolled, it wasn't pain I felt (for what was left to pain me?) but a sense of liberty. It didn't last.

2. Fields of clover, innumerable purple heads trapped inside stone walls, patterns in the wind, sun-ruffled, dark sycamores along the river and my Marie-Anne trailing her hands above the field, as if afraid to immerse them.

3. *La gabelle*, what a beast.

4. September light through the arched windows, the brass wheel and the weights, the small city of glass my instruments make.

5. Smell of sulfur, spark of phosphorus. The combustion lens cocked like a catapult, smoke pluming up in hot feathers.

6. When burned in air the products of combustion weigh more than the original.

7. Every quantity nests inside another larger measure (100 centimeters to the meter, 1000 meters to the kilometer);

8. and thus, my thumbnail, my arm, the lawn, the road to Paris lined with planted poplars.

9. When they came for me, they wouldn't speak my name, as if I had no longer had any weight.

10. Sun in *la Place de la Révolution*, the guttural crowd. I told Lagrange I would keep this up as long as possible.

11. The greased tower that holds the blade (the elegance of a machine well-designed, of course I recognize it.)

12. All I can hope is that someone is watching, that someone is keeping count.

13. The rim of the basket draped in oilcloth.

14. Crows.

DO YOUR POEMS BEGIN WITH
IMAGE OR EMOTION?

If image
is the beginning
then emotion is
sycamore
in St. Louis
(long avenues
of them), is
the river
thrumming against
the floodwall,
is the rain, is
the girl with wet
hair who watched
her mother die,
the cemetery
she never visits
beneath long
avenues of sycamore
that disappear
at the horizon
and end, finally,
in the pummel
of waves on a moon-
shaped shore
with evening
spread onto late

cloud cover,
so many cities
and countries
away from
the place—reach
for my hand
now is what
I would tell her,
as her keys flutter
and she arrives
at her building
below avenues
of sycamore—
where she began.

PINEME

The second angel taught the secret of writing and the use of pen and paper; thereby many
sinned from eternity to this day, because mankind was not created for such a purpose.

A's shape makes the roof of the house
I built for *B*—the pregnant woman.

C is the cup in despair, an archipelago of wine
splattered on the floor. *D* pilots the ship,

its sails belling with wind, and *E* becomes the shelves
whereon the ashes of my books doth lie.

F hooks her body from the past
as *G* traces the arc of the story as it returns *Home*.

I makes two columns of numbers
recorded in the ship's ledger—

the pen that writes our story and the chimney
long after the house has burnt to the ground.

J marks my turn away from God, and *K* is
the slings and arrows of outrageous forts.

L adds the boom to the mast that holds the sail
on the sea where *M* appears as islands rising from

the horizon, toothed against the setting sun.
N is now—the lonely hill above the valley, her grave—

and *O*, the far-seeing eye of God
that sees *P*, the quick sketch of a man, alone.

But *Q* is that eye with a log in it,
unwilling to see the speck.

R means another man stands naked before her.
S weeps as she boards the ship.

T tells us that *the end of all our exploring will be to arrive
where we started and know the place for the first time,*

but *U* holds the wine before it's spilled down
into *V*, our valley in this new world, green with loss.

W copies her breasts, the way they hung above me,
and *X* the shape our bodies made coming together.

Y is the divided way language moves through time
(I taught her this rough household of shapes)

and my open mouth yelling at the stars. *Z* waves
farewell and the ship zags back across the water.

WHAT IS POETRY? PART 1

A denned badger the dogs
don't smell and pass by.
Lithuania. Moxie. Jazz.

Bricks to chase the angels
out of the trees in the backyard.
A sprawl of men stacked

between girders like unread
books as the subway plunges
into Times Square station.

Rain and silence and rain.
Violet sabrewing at an empty feeder.
Tiny volcanoes that blow ash

onto deserted islands. Sunlight
and blue in the eye of a hurricane
fuming over Port Charles.

Test of endurance, measure of
abandon, rebellion, obsession; love-
song of the angels fleeing the trees.

The redheaded stepchild's
redheaded stepchild who becomes
the worst of all possible emperors.

FAKE NEWS

When Thucydides was young, he was sickly and small and could not compete with some of the older boys and so disgraced his small town of olive trees and hot rocks and goats and that sunlight like rage, and in their anger and his shame at their share in it, the boys held him down and pissed across his chest, and despite winning the boxing laurels and rising to the status of general years later, it seemed like nothing mattered except the feeling of heat on his chest like a hot sting. This is not true, or maybe it is true except his name was really Theo Clyde and the Greek village was a tar paper town in the Mississippi Delta and he was black and the boys were white and the piss was yellow and he would recall that hot rain of shame burning small holes in his chest as he beat a man nearly to death in the boxing ring later in his life.

Or maybe none of this is true
and the story here is the power
of words to make you think of
shame because that boy was
you. Or because the other boys
were you. Or both. Or neither.
And how, regardless, the words
ask you to carry them all—the
boy with small knives of urine
nicking his chest open and the
ones standing above him with
their dicks out for the world to
see like small tyrants.

BITCHES BREW

—Miles Davis

it's how angry a trumpet can be that makes
me want to talk about race in America
Miles said it was his dream to strangle
a white person talking about race is the cat
speaking on the question of mice or the cat
speaking on the question of dogs black like
the kids that stole my bike were black
and I was ten and came out from the store
to find them taking turns and riding in circles
on the sidewalk they laughed and I walked past
in silence and the words I choose mask my fear
with a different kind of fear in high school a white girl
took a black guy to prom and some kids made
a paper-mache cock six feet tall and left it
on her lawn in the dark of the night they left it
I knew who they were they were people
I called friends people who would do this
thirty years ago now I couldn't tell you
where one of them is or lives or works
ok one is a reformed alcoholic who can't drive
and walks everywhere around town that's all
I know I swear but I knew them then I knew
and said nothing who would I have told
the guy the girl the mother whose shrieks
opened the morning as she looked

across the lawn sound like Miles the pitch
of his horn working in a dark alley of cymbals
and snare and Chick Corea's keyboards
Bitches Brew was never played straight through
put together from sections of studio time
multiple keyboards and drummers mixed
with loops and reels and starts and stops hissing
and silence between you can't say it all at once
is what I'm saying and the pieces matter and
what you say matters and what you don't say
matters even more and when one friend
excused himself by saying he liked *black people*
but not niggers what I should have said
could fill this poem but what I did say can't
finish this line

ACHILLES IN JASPER, TEXAS

I know this: a man walked home drunk
along the corduroy of pines
in west Texas, the bronze duff,

dust and the late light that fell
on him. Three men gave him a lift

that afternoon and raised him
with their fists and lowered
him with their *nigger this* and

nigger that and after a while,
when all the fun they could have

with him leaked out into
the ruts of a logging cut,
they tied him to the boat

hitch of their truck and pulled
away. I know he kept his head up

awhile because his elbows were
ground to the bone; I know enough
was finally enough and his head

left his body behind,
but I don't know what to do

with this, America, this rage
like Achilles twitching
Hector behind his chariot

for twelve days until even
the gods were ashamed.

GADREEL

The third angel instructed the people in all the blows of death: how to make the instruments—the shield, the breastplate, and the sword for warfare.

Night herons come while the children are sleeping.
They come in the night, they do, with a feathering
of wings and their short, sharp beaks. They come

through the orange trees, faint hush of the Tigris.
In the small of the dark they come, they do.
Night herons come while the children are sleeping.

They step from the truck with a blossom of guns
into the orange orchards and the faint hush
of wings. With short, sharp beaks, they come

with a father and son. They come in the night, they do.
They step out of the truck, the headlights left on.
Night herons come while the children are sleeping.

In the small of the dark he is told
what to do. In the small of the dark he listens
to wings and their short, sharp beaks. They come

to shoot the informers. In the small of the night,
a father stands before his son. Puts a bullet in his eye.
Night herons come while the children are sleeping.
With wings and short, sharp beaks, they come.

SHARPSHOOTER

—Winslow Homer, oil on canvas

Blake saw, below the fire of willows
come autumn to SoHo, faces darkened

by coal-ruin and fog; he also saw
angels bespangling the beeches,

but in this pine, it's no angel balanced
against the branches—double-braced

with a boot against the trunk and hooked
in by the knee. He's blue in black and brown,

only a crimson patch coloring his cap
like the wing of a nested blackbird.

He waits for the rifle shot that arrives
in a shock across the fields of Sharpsburg.

The shine of his Whitworth Brass numbed
with mud. His eye to the scope eclipses

his own face in the long light of morning.
Anonymous as God, he watches and waits

until we come out of the woods.
We come marching and singing.

We come in motley and gray, smeared
like a gathering of fallen angels.

Before the shot, he searches our faces
in the gray and smoke as the fog

lifts its feathers off the Potomac.

DANTALION

The fourth angel is a man with many likenesses, which means the faces of all men and women. He teaches the arts and sciences and holds a book in one hand.

I wanted to talk about poetry today,
but there are 33 dead in Virginia.
Today someone is teaching a group
of children to hide in the closet. Someone
is passing out bulletproof blankets. I teach
all the arts and sciences but there are 33
dead in Virginia. I measured the sky.
I traced the way Virgil worms his way
into the modern epic. I talked this morning
about Julius Caesar crossing the Rubicon,
the way he paused and made camp
and how his soldiers stamped their feet
in the dark trying to keep warm.
I speak Latin. I speak French. I speak
Russian, Chinese, and Arabic.
I understand what it means when I talk
about quantum entanglement
and the flavors of quarks. I know quark
comes from Joyce (*Three quarks for
Muster Mark!*) and that *Finnegans Wake*
proceeds without a possessive. I know
the rules for the possessive and find
myself secretly hating those who don't.
I failed to sleep last night because I was

writing *Provide proof for your argument*
on one hundred papers. I was a small child
and shy. I rarely spoke. I lived in books
and paintings and saw the world reduced
today to the mouth at the end of a gun.
I was shot holding the door against a boy
so my students could drop from windows.
I was shot as I looked up from
my lecture. I was shot as I requested
my life. I walked with my eyes down,
beneath a sky measurably smaller.
I wanted to talk about poetry today.

WHAT ARE YOU READING?

I'm reading your book.
It's your range that attracts
me. You put a mirror between
two mirrors and imagine
the infinite and its opposite.
You lecture the bees
in the furious work
of their hive. You bell
the cat and mouse
down into a hole
in the wall, white as
a blank page. The way
you take risks, too,
like a wingwalker hung
from the stanchions
of a single-engine Bellanca,
buffeted by the wind of all
those open vowels, the electric
froth of the clouds now
above you, now below
and the plane dizzy
with your pyrotechnics,
I particularly admire. It's
all about danger, for you,
isn't it? The way you
stalk your poem through
the sea grass, filled like the sea

with all the plastic bangles
and coconuts jetsam
can manage, the long *V*
of the grass closing on
the heels of your poem
as it slips back toward
the trees and the small
house in the clearing
where you can still hear
the surf roughing up the
shore, and you, you predator
on after it. Now you
build beautiful contraptions
that snap shut around me,
now you let me free to
wander the trumpeting
fields of your imagination,
black-faced lambs nuzzling
clover, while you, like the
kindest of shepherds, start
the slaughter—your knife
the color of moonlight—so as
to lay out lunch for the wolf.

SHORT STORY FOR THE FBI

All eyes are upon you now
and everyone is listening—can't
you hear that clicking on the line?

That's the lonely detective
with his bag of chips. You know him
from a thousand film clips. He's waiting

for you to say something interesting,
waiting for you to say *bomb*
and not mean the club you hit

the night before where the lights
spun and zipped like carbonation
and the music was a second heart

in your chest and the girl with glitter
and smoked eyes like a Russian spy
touched your lips with her wrist

and misted away into the crowd.
But when you say it that way
you've dated yourself and the story's

not so fresh anymore, and
the detective has finished his chips
and he feels the lack of bourbon

precisely, and he desperately wants you
to hang up or incriminate yourself.
So, *tovarisch*, say something for him,

bring him into the lonely acre of your life.
Tell him a story, how once long ago you set
your house on fire with an aerosol can

and a bic, how the sudden union of
flame and curtain made you weep
until the fire brigade arrived, too late,

and—as the effervescence of their lights
flung itself into the faces of the dark
summer maples—stood around speculating.

SENTIMENTAL STANDARDS FROM THE AMERICAN CANON

I. *DIE HARD* OR THE ACTION-HERO POEM

would offer you a drink and a girl,
someone to get you through the night
since the honest stubble on its cheeks

says it's at least last call.
In all honesty, it knows you
will need someone to—at the last

desperate minute—untie the straps
when the flames unite your house
in a motif of blaze and ruin, gas can

empty on the floor next to the chair
and your scattered Tito Puente albums.
Knows you will need someone to take

full command of being in jeopardy
and shrieking, later, when the big boss
makes revenge his major project

from the burrow of his industrial lair
into which you will descend like Dante
with a bad haircut and a hangover,

ladders and catwalks cinematically perfect
for minions to fling themselves from. Since
it's clear you need someone to make you risk

risk, someone to be a crack in the foundation
of your chiseled heart. Because this isn't
the Western Poem and you can't be Shane

riding off into the fragile ecosystem
of your own lonely egotism any more.
It asks that you walk into the shallow cave

of this genre and wait to be manhandled.
Honestly, the boss will tell you everything
after the punishment begins, don't worry.

All you have to do is take the smackdown
and endure, to encourage the fists to find
your face and blood to express itself

across the plaster, take it
and *come back, come back* for more,
since that's your main (let's be honest) skill.

II. THE COUNTRY-WESTERN POEM

knows that first there is the matter
of your gargantuan patriotism
brandishing the stars and bars

of its own obstinate self-regard
to explore before the ekphrasis
of the pickup and the shotgun and

the reddog beside you is addressed—
triptych of American exceptionalism—
before you can come to the girl

in the halter and the Daisy Dukes,
that sass-talking schoolmarm
crossed with pole-dancer ingenue.

She will be waiting by the tracks that
tie up the landscape in glorious ribbons
of unending steel that ride on across

levies and soybeans, drop slow grades
and run beside rivers flowing deeply
as money into the consciousness

of a country too big for itself, a mess
of space and light going in and out
of black-and-white, the grainy

retrospective Americana of the split rail
and the water tower and the snapping flags
that refer back to the opening acts

of this little drama of a nation as the light
turns golden in the west across the ticking
of the corn. She'll be waiting to take you

into the honky-tonk accommodation
of her quite heaving bosom, forever
waiting to drive with you into a sunset

that glows like the flags and flames decal
in the window of the back of your truck—
the huge Hemi of it heaving and sobbing.

III. THE FILM NOIR POEM

would—after the second bottle
of the white Côtes du Rhône
and the black sack of clams shelled

to a ruin of half-moons on the floor
as the wind eats the trees and the rain
salts the tin roof hard, the air like brine—

find you hollow as a foxhole, sipping
from a hip flask, just before you have to fight
your way out of the double-double-cross

of your own desire. It knows what you want—
closure and denouement—but it knows, too,
that you are nothing but hunger. Knows you

grow larger as you swallow the mob boss,
his white suit and the shadowy thugs, too,
the chiaroscuro of the abandoned sound stage,

but there is no satiety. You will consume
the world and the script, ravenous,
the whole damn film in your wet-lipped

hunger. You will eat until your life
is a bucket of empty shells, wine bottles
like grenades tossed at your feet.

IV. THE MURDER MYSTERY POEM

knows who did it with the candlestick
on the train of itself running the long night
through to the Orient expressly for the purpose

of discovering all that it knows already:
the who-done-it-ness of the pistol
on the mantle waiting for the lights

to come down and moment to be pregnant enough—
and *pregnant enough* is enough of a motive isn't it,
really?—for the shot in the dark, for the knife

that shines wickedly and winks from the flashlight
carried into every car on this damn train, running on
and on with the front visible from the back now

as it takes the bend in the mountains. But
the second class are passengers revolting
(*They certainly are*, says the poem, sniffing)

against the intent of all this intrigue
that would have them killed off one by one
like so many redshirts in the Science Fiction Poem.

At this point the plot should have thickened like tar,
like the bubble and stench of the creosote banter
of the—where the hell is that detective anyway?

He's shellacked in the back with the comic
relief, the whole story turned to sitcom.
They're passing a bottle back and forth

and singing into the drawn-out night
the train tunnels through because
he has long ago given up hope

of discovering the villain who opens
the door to the tiny washroom,
and sees *your* face in the mirror

stroking and stroking the foam
from the delicate skin of your throat with
a straight razor's long and elegant blade.

IN THE TOWN CALLED CLICHÉ

the baker makes thirteen of everything
and the candlestick maker can't

keep his double-wicked candles in stock
but the butcher is reduced to selling

the horse he rode in on. The kids
fall from the apple trees and roll

over the hill and the laundress
hangs three sheets from the roof

of the local pub as the village idiot
pushes daisies down the street

in his cart. His horse, of course,
follows. When the Pope came

to town and had to shit, he went
into the woods and was promptly

eaten by a bear, but, today, dogs
and cats lie together in puddles of sun

after all the hard rains of spring
and, while many hands work lightly

pitting bowls of cherries—devilishly
diligent people, industrious as owls—

the only road out of town is paved with
good intensions and the mayor throws stones

from the balcony of his glass house,
yet he dresses in the basement.

PERSONAL

Tall café mocha
looking for plain
black decaf.

Thick-necked man,
snores like a sick hog.
Seeks deaf woman,
lip reading a plus.

Woman who speaks
only English needs man
who speaks only Spanish.
No talking during the movie.

Bisexual cowboy seeks same.

Man who distills own vodka
from purple fingerling
potatoes seeks woman
who can drink him
under the table.

Man who has failed
at everything he's tried
seeks woman
who doesn't know

the meaning of failure.
Let me teach you.

Small brains, small
chest. Looking for a man
with low standards.

Poet in need of praise.
Lie to me, please.
I pay by the word.

Just like your mother,
I'll be disappointed
whatever you do.
Please call, &
don't forget to eat.

JOKES

I.

As the joke begins, a doe walks
out of the forest and the trees
time-lapse up into the sky and
ferns unfiddle in the sudden fog.
The doe steps out of the forest
and shakes her head, blocky
and big-eyed. She labors into
the numb bracken. The doe
steps out of the forest,
shakes her head and says, *God*,
and a pole of light breaks through
the fog and pins her to the gap
in the trees she has just made.
The doe steps out of the forest,
shakes her head and says, *God*,
I'll never do that again, and the trees
behind her apron a litter of bottles.

II.

Two guys lost in the woods
stumble upon a giant hole
in the narrative and stop
their discussion about the doe

that stepped out of the woods
and begin tossing things down
the hole, because that's what
a hole demands, after all
(the center of the story,
the vortex where all things
come together and miss).
And when they've dropped
all they can find into the hole
and no sound echoes up
from the bottom of that space
to fill the hollowness inside,
they set off in a search
of something heavy enough
to fill the hole with noise,
and what they find is
a railroad tie and they cart it
over and toss it in. Fortunately
for them, just then, a goat
sprints out of the brush,
pumping its origami legs,
and dives into the hole.
They stand bent as wet grass
looking down into the hole
hoping to find some answers
to all the questions that arise
from a silent hole filled with nothing
and a goat. Just then a farmer
shambles up and says in his accent
ripe as rotten pears, *Hey, you boys
seen a goat around here?*

III.

Two guys (two different guys,
mind you; the first two

are still staring down
into a hole in the woods

and wondering about the farmer
and what, if anything, they should say

about the goat that dove
into their lives and the hole in it)

two guys walk into a bar.
The third one ducked.

IV.

A duck walks into a bar,
blue head gleaming and plumes
the mottle of sun-worn asphalt,

says to the bartender:
*Hey, you seen my brother
around here?*
                    And the bartender
looks at the duck for a minute,
then says, *Well what he look like?*

V.

Two guys, a duck, and a goat walk into a bar.

Bartender says, *What is this, some kind of joke?*

VI.

And so the farmer says, *You two boys
seen my goat around here?*

And the two guys say, *Well, there was
this goat just a minute ago ran up
and dove right in this hole.*

VII.

The duck shakes his blue head,
smoothes his plumes the color
of gravel. The goat says
nothing, goes on saying
nothing as he falls forever
down a hole. In saying nothing
the goat says all that needs to be
said about a hole in the woods.

VIII.

And the farmer says, *Nah, that weren't my goat.
My goat's tied up to a railroad tie.*

IX.

The two guys finally find
their way out of the woods
and into a bar planked
with pine and windows
full of the small light
that struggles through
the trees. Two does
shoulder through
frames above the bar.
They turn their heads
expectant in the fragrant
air, eyes dead as dice.

The two guys are sick
of jokes and the hole
at the middle of each one,
sick of the duck and
his vanity, the goat
who now kneels down
in the corner, content
to be doing anything
other than falling forever
down a hole. Unable

to resist, one guy
finally says to the other,
So this doe walks out
of the woods, shakes
her head and says, "God,
I'll never do that again
for two bucks." Nobody

laughs. They order
a shot and a beer and sit
drinking the heart out
of the bright spring day.

MAINE ROOM

—Andrew Wyeth, watercolor and graphite on paper

It's the late light that gouges
at the heart, really. November's end
and the leaves down. Birch trunks
and the calligraphy of shade.
Cold light, clean light. In a square
of it, wooden plovers on the mantle
preen in a room so Spartan
it could be being punished for
something, the way the woods
in winter are punished with snow
in a thin light that warms nothing,
the way the wind channels down
through the gaps in the mountains
and finds the hearth of the sea
cold and dark in some room
abandoned somewhere and empty.

ELEGY IN PURPLE

*. . . and then Jesus cried out again in a loud voice, he gave up his spirit. At that
moment, the curtain of the temple was torn in two from top to bottom.*

—MATTHEW 27:50-51

u sexy motherfucker

—PRINCE

The squeal Prince makes in the middle
of "Little Red Corvette" after crooning,

You got an ass like I never seen,
is untranslatable—wet guitars mating

with the wind, grief coming alive
in an engine's reverb, 8 cylinders

of desire smoothed down with the blush
of 1,000 roses—so there is only silence

this morning. Outside the sky lies
a high weeping blue across the world

and rotten snow wanders back alleys
of shadow. The day is cold and new

and the rest of the song gets lost
in the wind and the bustle and wrack

of passing traffic. The white doves
of the clouds turn into questions

that have no answers, the way his falsetto
careens into heavy breathing, the backbeat,

and Lisa's raw vocals. His eyes like hot
welcome, his cheekbones shaved ice.

I am not going to talk about a boy
worshipping that bass and glide,

so full of wanting in my room of books
and fat speakers, desire's iconography

playing out every day on my TV,
the shine of sleek bodies and fame.

It's just this sound beguiles me, even now:
the unloosening of desire, the flowering lovecry

of angels who came to earth to seduce
with James Brown hips and licks wicked

as his grin, the elegant, enamored purpling
of the air with spring rising across the world

like a man alone in the spotlight
just before the curtain is torn apart.

LUSH LIFE

—Chet Baker

This late in his life he looks less
like James Dean than the late Lowell,
playing Hop Singh's, mouth sunken

from that drug scuffle, 50's fame
and adulation (the girls who
washed across his limo like a surf

of flowers vanished) and what's left
is the ache of his take on "Lush Life."
It seems easy to say heroin

caused all this, but that's too simple.
I don't know enough about him
to write it but I am trying because I hear

in that horn a voice stretching after
something that in some storefront in
some broken town might resemble

happiness, the way the arch of the bridge
across the river at the town's dusty edge
resembles freedom. Freeman's chords

are a raft he might use to cross over
but each time he approaches the edge
and looks into the water that has

only stars reflected in it—their small
stammer, the rest of the world and
the trees darker still—the song floats on.

There's a garden here in Amsterdam,
filled with black-eyed Susan and lupine
like a minor key, and the window

where he will learn gravity's major lesson,
but all that's to come. There's still time
for the light from the Dutch transom

to cross the wall, but there's nothing
I can do to keep it from happening
and no one saves anyone

anyway. Still, there's something in
his performance that says he'll stay all day
in that tall room with wind ghosted in

on blurry curtains, shooting up, ruining
everything with cigarettes and the sound
of something resembling happiness.

AIN'T MISBEHAVIN'

—Nixon and Armstrong, 1952

In the buzzy neon and fresh vinyl of LAX,
two men come together, the senator from California

and a trumpet player; they come together around
the spinning black track the baggage claim

makes and grip each other's hand and
for a moment look like a photo and its negative.

I'm a big fan, says Nixon, smiling rich
as cream, *if there's ever anything I can do for you,*

just let me know. And to the surprise of everyone,
Armstrong shuffles his eyes down, replies,

Well, suh, I got an extra bag an' if you could grab it
I'd be grateful. And everyone's watching now and now

Nixon's grin falls a little
but he's a little too good at his job

to be rattled and snatches the bag and carries it
through customs while the merry snickers

of the band follow him the way a wake follows a boat
into the dock. A blue marl of sky clouds the glasses

of the men who stand sentry around the senator
as the two men move toward the black silk

of their limos and Armstrong opens up
his picket-fence smile and accepts the bag back

with a shuck and a nod to the other layers
of the story, race riots and war, the thicket

of heat rising up the manzanita hills, lies ready to brushfire
their way through the American experience. And given

all he was and all that will happen—black-capped
burglars with their satchels, wiretaps hissing on the line—

I'm only too happy to show you Nixon humiliated here,
but who's to say that's the story; the future's still

blank as the glasses of the senator's men.
A circus of hands gathers the bags and stacks them

in the trunks of cars as the sunlight sloughs off
the twin aircraft parked nose to nose in the blooming heat.

Nixon knew what it meant to make a man a fool, but
Armstrong knew customs would never

search the senator and find the quarter pound
of Jamaican Pearl he'd hidden in that bag.

STOP MAKING SENSE

Hi. I got a tape I want to play you.
—DAVID BYRNE

Before the Big Suit, and
and the 80s keyboards,
before the naïve melodies,
there were white shoes
and a boom box, an empty
stage unaccompanied by thought
and all its paraphernalia
and Byrne rattling around
with his acoustic and
tripping to the gunshot
beat—awkward chicken,
white Kabuki—there was
me in the crowd at 17,
thinking in the dark
chairs (a little high,
honestly) about honesty
and believing it to be art,
and all the while nothing
happened outside:
wind raw in the trees,
the road flint-colored
and splattered with the
marquee's scatter of white.

It's all artificial of course.
Even the drum beat from
the boom box as it sets
time for the acoustic jags
of Byrne's guitar as he
rustles around the ladders
and rafter-climbers and
the stagehands drag
the risers from the wings,
song by song, each selection built
so that when the band gathers,
so when Byrne finally comes out
in the Big Suit . . . No, no,
it's not time for that yet.

Instead, I come back to the way
an audience becomes itself
in the articulation of
its desire to be the music,
to me in the dark with
the radiance of the crowd
streaming from us.
I come back to my self
in the dark growing
and the orchestration that
captures all the trappings
of thought and thinking
that becomes me
as I watch Byrne
in the Big Suit jerk
and herkle the crowd with
his masquerade that's more
real for being live on stage.

The growl and squeak,
the seamless in-and-out
motion of the dancers
that becomes thought visible:
white bird on the wing,
runners on treadmills
approaching nowhere.

for Dan Gunn

WHAT IS POETRY? PART 2

The light
that points
the way

in the fog.
The light
in the fog

that thickens
and reveals
the fog's

cold breath.
The fog
as well.

TELEGRAPH GHAZAL

At first you might suspect news of an unstoppable
gold rush in the South Dakota hills. But that's not it. Stop

thinking of all the mines turning stone to smoke and the greasy
water that slips out in cyanide and cadmium from the stopped-

up gullies. Or news that great-aunt Mabel, known only to you
in the small yellowing of some photos, has stopped

breathing and you, as the only next-to-next-of kin, are the one
to collect her. This is not the way we communicate now. Stop.

We expect the Amazonian link where our books are forever for sale
in the evergreen forest of commerce. The attached video with nonstop

girl-on-girl action. It's all a-Twitter.
It's about branding, don't you Digg it? Stop

it for chrissakes, won't you, Thomson? Haven't you made your point?
Now that we're connected, there's nothing that can stop us.

FORNEUS

*The last angel teaches rhetoric and languages, gives men a good
name, and makes them beloved by their friends and foes.*

This is historic times. I think we can agree
the past is over. It is a time of sorrow and
sadness when we lose a loss of life. There's
no question that the minute I got elected
the storm clouds on the horizon were getting
nearly directly overhead. Make no mistake
about it, I understand how tough it is, sir.
I talk to families who die. Families is where
our nation finds hope, where wings take dream.
I tell people, let's don't fear the future, let's shape it.
One year ago today, the time for excuse-making
has come to an end. We cannot let terrorists
and rogue nations hold this nation hostile.
Security is the essential roadblock to
achieving the road map to peace. And
I just want you to know that, when we talk
about war, we're really talking about peace.
The only way we can win is to leave
before the job is done. I promise you
I will listen to what has been said here,
even though I wasn't here. I am a person
who recognizes the fallacy of humans.
They have miscalculated me as a leader—
when I am talking about myself and

when he's talking about myself, all of us
are talking about me. See, in my line of work
you've got to repeat things over and over
and over again for the truth to sink in, to kind
of catapult the propaganda. Anybody
who is in a position to serve this country
ought to understand the consequences of words.

THIS HAS BEEN A TEST OF THE
EMERGENCY BROADCAST SYSTEM

Had this been a true emergency
there would have been the sound of

falling rubble and bowing girders.
There would have been blare and clash,

ruckus and mortuary work.
There would have been symphonic want

and multisyllabic heartbreak, banner headlines
and bandwagons. Had this been a true emergency

you would have been directed to breathe
in the smoke from the lingering fires

of all the speeches that reference this day.
There would have been soldiers sent

and garrisons, oil and tents, rifles black
as snouts. Roughing up. Electrodes

and hoods. There would have been a man
thrown from a helicopter. Genuflecting

and orchestras and roundups, yes, and hoodlums
rumbling through the streets in vast, gassed-up militias

of the night. There would have been
the illusion of control. Fear of suitcases.

A ban on ball bearings. A new architecture
based on Kevlar and concrete and

the absence of windows that will not
be missed. Had this been a true emergency

there would have been caskets and a run
on flags. Sniggering and something about a zoo.

Razor wire and tent camps. Sealed roads
that lead into tumbleweeds, the small clutch

at the roots as the wind takes them.
There would have been loneliness and wicked

nostalgia. In the mountains where no one
will be allowed there would have been

an accumulation of snow like an unending
series of predictions. But, there would have been

no warning. Have a nice day.

THE HALO BRACE
(SELECTED SECTIONS)

(1998)

The afternoon closed over
in sheets of rain, unopened
by the words spread out
on the page, the air heavy

and attentive to the press
of flesh in silhouetted rooms.
They spoke in whispers,
sibilant vocables, liquid

sound on the windows. And
by the bed a book of poems
opened to Rilke's address
to Orpheus (she had read

aloud to him)—We are already
free, and were dismissed
where we thought we would soon
be at home—and a threshold

opened in the ruined trees.
A semblance of grief in clothes
spread across the floor and
loss opened by the name of loss.

1.

The Easter bells at Hitt and Locust,
the knell sounding along the rim of elms,
mean for me the death of love—

a woven cloth of air and a wealth
of oriels winding through.
As a cup raised in thanksgiving

means the absence of a language
to express what has become of us,
so desire become desire,

a tongue tastes tongues of air.
This music is the music I hear
desiring you. A weave of birds

through the smoking morning trees,
a thread of leaves disturbs the ground:
a shroud, a web of birds, this woven sound.

II.

A man gesturing. A woman holding back. This is the image
that remains. A man motioning in anger, his arms quick,
        his gestures severe.

A woman turned inward.

Or was it the other way? A woman's quick anger? A man's
        distance.

They stand together, connected in the emotion called up
        with the scene.
The exist only together. A man and a woman.

Above them, the elms weep yellow leaves.

III.

How did we get here, through the morning into a streaked biography of trees?

That day, she sits in the halo of a reading lamp, the page a glare of white in the bright sunlight that descends through the library windows. He sits across from her. Their talk is nervous, each unsure what worlds to inhabit with the other, what words to use to make a world. He asks her to read to him. She opens Borges, reads the imagined garden, and so he imagines Buenos Aires for her. Together they walk past the esplanade into the streaking traffic—amber and cardinal swerving around *la Obelisc*—towards *Teatro Colon* for coffee.

v.

Those nights I tended bar, riverside
on the Illinois, watching the searching
spotlights on the working barges
blaze across the deck chairs and
then drop everything back into shadow;
they shuddered upstream furrowing
the slack, reflecting water. The days
were wide and hot that summer, no rain.

Bank doors slapped in the heat
and as we passed we were reflected
in the wavering gold, the whiskey-
colored glass that gave us back
our dry world, ghostly and fluid.

You should fall in love more often.

This woman with rain-dark hair
who came to my bed and left it wet,
a faint leaf-pattern spreading.
I would touch her face with the back
of my hand and watch her walk
to the kitchen for water,

the small cups of her breasts blue
in a light that quickly faded.
But those were days when I was always drunk
and such grace never lasted long.

VII.

In a city named for a king, for a distant, lost king whose heart was ruined under a surge of freedom, who looked into the broken sky and could not, finally, understand the new world, he watched her walk away, the wet cobblestone streets, the mist at night like old phantom houseboats of jazz. (There is something in her in that moment that he cannot understand, a confidence, an arrogance, though he would surely find that word *inexact*, somehow.) Nighthawks cut the sky to pieces and in whispers cars hiss across a city cut with bridges. The river flows south here, a muddy surge of knowing, and the girders of the MLK hum in gentle earnestness, a reverb that he feels even now echo in the soles of his feet, in the airy vibration of foxglove in a burned lot of shadow and rubble. It is true that the heart learns through sorrow, but not that the heart knows nothing more than sorrow.

VIII.

Her hair gathered on her head, J. bends to the long bench with the weight of her shoulders, the sandpaper a creased map in her cramping fingers, the hair on her arms frosted with her work. A pew we rescued from a burned church. The small country church burned out. We pulled it off the lawn below the smoke-haloed windows, water damaged and stinking of creosote.

Months later she will hold my head between her thighs as I tongue open the lush spice of her sex. She moans and arches her back to me, the pew sanded smooth, rich with stain. It is dangerous to want something this much. She bends again and again, the dark satin retreating beneath her hands, small wings of sweat forming between her shoulders.

XII.

A chokecherry full of cedar waxwings, they gorge themselves on winter fruit. Their gold-gone-gray is the color of the season.

A woman's dark hair purls across her pillow and her eyes, far gone in pleasure.

To paint the color of rain, painters used ground pumice mixed with rust and quicksilver. It was expensive and thus rare in use.

Firdausi, the great Persian poet exiled at 25, wandered Assyria reciting his *Shah Namah*, returning home only to die.

There are three things capable of wrecking love.

The hanging fruit in Juan Cotan's *Still Life*—lit by a golden light from beyond the frame—form a perfect parabola rising to the right.

To paint the color of sunlight at noon, mix gypsum with the pollen of tickseed sunflowers and ground abalone.

The scudding whirl of birds across the burned-back, aubergine fallow, the crusted broken wheat, the cut leaves of chicory and cheat whipped in the wind. The trees are a monotone fence line. The birds, their wings, bright as they turn away.

A bridge through marsh sawgrass, the cattails bobbing with redwings.

In ancient India, Vishnu could not create the world until he had caught the great fish which had swallowed the book of knowledge.

XIII.

When the final storm of summer
swept into Chicago and the sky
blanched to a languid jaundice,
we walked from Lake Michigan
and, finally home and streaming
with rain, ended on the floor
of her cold-water flat
in a curled sixty-nine while
the sky was a wrinkled net
of lightning, the low ceiling
holding us close, this dark warren
heavy with breath. Each slick
with the other, we slept there
on the floor only to wake
with the wet air aureoled
around the streetlights, halogen
coronas running to Dearborn.
There is more, yet, to this telling,
tender details that might ignite
the small petals of jasmine
I pressed between the pages
of Hikmet: *You are my city,*
most beautiful and most unhappy.

XV.

The rain was long and hard that fall,
daily gray the Illinois filled and rose

below the barges, the lights faintly streaked
upon the water. As we had quarreled

in the wet dusk grown large,
the remaining day mottled with dark leaves,

I knelt at the low window expecting J.
to stalk down the wet walk, but instead

she came quietly to me, a cupped hand
across my cheek. *I love you.*

Her eyes were wet, her hair was dark
and her answer came in a heavy breath:

I know, she said. *I've known for weeks,
but I was afraid to tell you.* In the window

the last remaining elm was bare; its leaves
had fallen early. They would be gold

across the grass if they hadn't soured
already—brown, sodden and rutty—

and what did I know of love when the one
I loved feared to speak those words to me?

XVI.

Tell me a story, she says. In a long hall, a library which is a world, there are shelves that recede out of sight. The books are heavy and the room smells of oil and human hair. A man steps to the shelf marked with a gothic *J*. He lifts a book from the wall. The loose spine sighs open.

He places a finger on a line of text. A Tuscan villa appears gnarled with dry ivy, the winter bare fronds of dark willows. The world that is the text. He moves his hands and flames open the windows, heave into the sky. He pulls his hands back and the trees fill with leaves. The text that is the world.

He runs his finger down the page until a woman appears, thin, her arms striped with smoke. He says to her, "Come with me." Without a word, she moves with him out the door. He is holding the book always before him as he walks with her into a morning light the color of her name.

XVII.

A cold-water flat lit by a plate of fruit.
A dog disheveling the trash out back,
rotten meat, rinds, empty bottles of wine.
J. lies about the room. Outside,
bright houseboats line the harbor, taut
water reflecting the sky. What J. does here
will change everything. She will leave and
walk down the alley. She will buy a small clock
in a shop near the cathedral. How can I explain?
The day becomes a still life, now, as I recall it,
and J. is frozen there. Her clock, fretworked,
scrolled in walnut, holds the table open:
books, a pair of folded spectacles,

a plate of d'anjou pears. The late afternoon
light, as in Caravaggio's *Christ*, shadows
the bed behind her. Christ's torso beneath
the angled light. His beautiful equanimity.
Thomas's finger thrust into his wounded side.
The hands of the clock hold four forty-five.
How she must wish to move, but I can hardly bear
to imagine what happened. And I won't. Let it
suffice, the mad rage for movement arrested

in this moment. Caravaggio's heavy lips,
the dark mat of hair, tortured and turned under
his sweating palms. The rain-wet streets of Rome.
The man he killed in quarrel bleeding at his feet.

XVIII.

This is what he loves about her, even now, the small hollow at her neck, the moon-shaped cup inside her elbow, her lips when she reads poetry aloud, and the way her lips move quickly from anger into love. Her wit. The way her body holds his steady, like river sand, beneath him.

XIX.

The clams we ate, tossing
their small lunar shells into a pail,
their liquid, tongued bodies
swirled in garlic and butter,
pearl onions and wine, are easier
to recall than what happened
after—the sex turning sour.
We fucked in anger, and more,
our bodies cold arenas
for the words we wouldn't say,
or wouldn't say until later.
Still, the jacaranda outside
the window—its whorish musk
and lavender, funneled corollas—
paints the scene an amorous hue,
and the bucket of small moons
on the floor, whole worlds
for us to conquer.

xx.

I.
At Snowdrift Lake, I dreamt of bears,
the moon orange in the saddle of Whister,
the elk hole sage gold below, beyond
the drainage of Avalanche Canyon;
lumbering through my sleep—
oso, ours, Ursidae, bera—through
the jackpines and wet heather
of the misted Wind Rivers where
we had passed and J. was teaching
me Chinese, all tone and intonation:
Kao shan. Mountains. *Yeuh*. Moon.
Zhen. Precious, treasure, pearl.

But what if this were all lie
made in her absence? What if
I camped alone and was afraid,
the moon sterling and the lunar ruin
of stone marked with dirt-gray glaciers?
Would it suffice? A bear framed against
the lichen-striped rock, lithograph
black and checking the air.

II.

Bai ju, she says. Moonshine.
Beishung. Shadow bear. Panda.
Perhaps together we camped
in the damp shadow of arrow bamboo,
clustered among the knuckled roots,
rhododendrons clumped with snow
and drank what we could
from a farmer's jug of homebrew.

Mao, mao, mao, mao, she says.
Hair, cat, plentiful, rust.
How easily it all slips, word by word
by tone. Now the moon is rust and
snowdrift is mantled with plentiful fog.
Pandas shamble through the juniper,
cat quiet. And I am no longer dreaming.
I have left the poem, but J.
is still there mouthing the words,
passing over roads spread out like hair.
I have left the poem in her hands:
Tang, tang, tang, tang, she says.
She says, sugar, soup, hot, if.

XXI.

I am made of the words you are writing,
she says as I cup her breast, tongue her
nipple. Her legs are braided in mine.
Epidermis, I say, *breast, bread, bowl.*
The bed is wet with moonlight and cars
hiss pass. *You need to ask my permission,*
next time.

XXIV.

There is a sound that rises
every dawn, the morning windows

striped with light,
that is the sound of rustling grain.

J.'s hair, dark gray and blackish brown,
rain's color on aisles of asphalt,

shifts and pours across the pillow,
dark star, black petals. My whole life

I have heard this sound: the wind
in the winter sycamore rattling

curled leaves, the long sharpening of knives.
I loved this sound before I knew

it came from her, in hornets caught
in blue flowers, in snow ticking

iced glass, and the marvelous hum
of our cells counting down, dividing,

dying. Come with me, listen quietly.
The sound I love is the sound

of my love moving, water flowing,
a spadeful of dirt returning to the earth.

XXVI.

All day, in a thin stinging drizzle,
they've torn the street back from itself
with groaning hydraulics—all
elbows—the metallic ringing thud
of the backhoe hammering into
the pavement. Squatting machines
rake ingots of concrete into the air
exposing the wet, sucking earth.

And then the question comes,
as it must, where is the meaning here?
And how does one make a certainty
of our various lives? This is a *story*,
after all, of how J. happened
into a space of meaning. How love's
an absence we pour ourselves into
in a luxury of construction, then
an ache of wreckage—violent as rain.

xxx.

A murmur of rain
through the open door,

the long math of argument,

ambulance lights caught
in Ball jars of lilac—

beautiful as Lucifer,

named for light,
who fell and knew hell

as hell himself

falling. *What is
your substance, whereof*

are you made

*that millions of strange
shadows on you tend.*

Fern breaks, banded moss,

a ripple of birds
on weathered grass.

What I have said

has darkened your face.
In the wind, the clematis

rises, plashing its blue fists against

the glass, as the wet petals
of my irises droop

and make the shadows

of penance in this,
their garden.

XXXI.

This the hour when the water on the land
still holds the light of day and a heavy dark
moves in the trees along the river. J. coaxes

words from me—*palette, river, moon*—
but there are other words she would rather hear.
Far from here, far upstream, where the river thins

and is riffled with rocks, a shallow faith is born
among cattails and quick river birds, a faith
in water that drags us down to rivers,

to estuaries and coastlines, a spirit level of grass
along the dark bay. We share a language of water.
We make a poetry of absence. *The kind of poetry*

I want is my love who comes back with the rain.
The kind of poetry I want is the wet grass
in January, the word yellow in the mouth of a dove.

Again, I tell her: *the flat palette of a winter sunset,*
light remaining on the river and a thumbnail moon
hung among wind-stripped sycamores.

XXXV.

palindrome [Gr. palíndromos *running back again]*

Can you imagine the joy
of the hand reaching out of the dust
into sickness, slowly, into health?

And mourners who no longer mourn—
the crowd around the grave welcomes
this, their kind of birth. The wrinkled

skin puckered back across the cheeks
suddenly taut, a sail in sudden wind.
Can you imagine? The crumpled body

rising from the trough of the wreck, blood
and shattered glass. Children tunneling
back into the bodies of our loves

as we fumble into kisses and touch
each other's awkward faces. Above the autumn
trees, sugar maples flaming, sallow larch

arching over the dark creek, there is
a swirl of buzzards circling backwards
and we are somehow growing out of love.

XXXVII.

And the stars on Madeline Island, the bend
of the galaxy. J. is on her back
in the wet grass, our tent on the dark
granite shore. We're looking for twin
systems: Andromeda, its low ascension,
and Sirius, its dark companion at apastron held.
The wind off Superior in August is cold;
the shore is wet with spray. All's illusion.
We are splitting up. She lies in the grass
and says, *I don't move you anymore.*
And I can no longer stand to imagine a world
where she would. I'm at my desk. The 11:05 bus
has passed. The morning's been torn;
afternoon's long turn toward evening unfurls.

XXXVIII.

A man and a woman bent apart by the joke he tells to a friend. The two men laugh loudly in the echoing library. She passes by; he hears only a chair scrape the floor in a long hall. She settles at a table crowned by a reading lamp's corona in the failing dusklight reading Borges: *a book which does not contain its counterbook is considered incomplete.*

XLI.

Again argument. When J. left
the door swung shut behind her

in a reminiscence of loss,
the maples scalloped with color,

dust rising along the long path
of the drive. But no,

it wasn't that way. It was morning
and a thin mist aged the thin leaves,

the asphalt wet with rain.
Everything was gray and smelled

of horses, an appaloosa dawn.
But it wasn't that way either.

She left a message on the table—
It's inevitable—and suddenly it was.

XLII.

Trains ran through my dreams those nights—
the sobbing language of their horns
echoing in the autumn that arrived
in a scarf of clouds along the horizon,
the call of jays in the Osage orange.
I woke alone in the days after J. left,
I woke to an apartment damaged
by space, to words like *forgiveness*
and *remorse* trailing along the floorboards.
And I read again the words of John,
who was not the light but the envoy
of the light, whose perfect Christ wrote
his only text with a finger in the Galilee sand,
and effaced it with a gentle, trailing hand.

XLIII.

When J. called from Houston to tell me she'd been hurt, we hadn't spoken in years. She woke in the ICU, half the bones in her body broken, her spleen gone, and her flesh zippered with scars. Screwed into her skull, a cage around her face—a halo brace—protection for whatever grace remains. She taught herself to walk again, spliced bones webbing whole.

I want to ask her why she's called but my question comes out wrong. It's nothing I could have guessed, she says. Out to dinner, I looked left, looked right; that black pickup came out of nowhere. Long days later, sitting drinking coffee, she watched a young boy stop traffic with his walk. The cars all paused to let him pass. They would have bowed if they could.

XLIV.

Five sketches drawn in her absence:

—Heavy chevrons of Canada geese against the wide palette of the west, collapsing across a sunset pond rimmed with alders.

—A man cupping an enormous leaf in the honeycombed subways under Washington.

—A fragile shelf of light at the horizon beyond the mist-wrapped verge of the Bitterroots, the long rainbow of dawn. On the table a bottle, half vodka/half light.

—In Vermeer's *Woman Holding a Balance*, her eggshell hood is illumined in a shaft of sun beaded with light, and the gold scale held in her small, articulate hands. On the wall behind her, an anonymous, dark *Judgement*: the flat, dim silhouettes of the damned.

—Her face turned away from mine, turned toward dusk and the imperfect tendency of language to survive.

XLV.

It is worse, he thinks, that he never saw her there, in that nest of wires and tubing, the bruise-blue web connecting the shattered arch of her cheek and the aquiline motion of her ear circled with dark hair. Unseen, she becomes everything wrecked in his life: bone-chipped, broken porcelain on the table or the heron that curled across the prairie highway—its rain-gray feathers soaked with the azure of the distant sky—and crossed the semi's path, exploding in a bulging whirl of feathers and legs, eddies in the coughing exhaust.

XLVI.

Speech after silence, silence, rain
from yellow clouds as mountains billow.
The tarmac sizzles, August air. J. descends
from her plane, her hair is longer now.
As we come together, a kiss, a small reunion.
We maunder up into the hills beyond San José,
rising to Cartago and through, falling towards
the Caribbean. The fields are burning,
the fields of sugarcane, black acrid earth.
The road is a shroud. *Will you turn your head
across your far shoulder?* I've crossed
the char-dark earth. The fields are burning,
the fields lost in smoke and our minds' own sunset,
the dark unfolding hills behind us in the west.

XLVII.

Above the hills, forgotten stars are obscured
by clouds. Night falls in a broken crest of rain,
drawing arrows on the pavement.

J. shakes her hair and the chandelier
casts stars upon the walls. The clock's hands
arrow near the hour. A green light reigns.

Time's arrow flows either way—*Remember*
the shooting stars on Madeline Island
that autumn?—and memory is an open door.

They were a kind of light, a kind of rain.
They are not rain. *The hair of stars, then?*
Star-light wire. They are not light, not rain.

And not the tree-flocked sparrows
waiting out the storm. The floorboards
in the narrow hall, sallow light on the hanging

photographs. J. and I and a doorway
between us. *Rain-dark hair.*
Forgotten stars. What *is* is spoken.

In the wet dusk, her words fall and fall.
Soft hair, brisk arrows.
Somewhere it is raining stars.

XLVIII.

Those were the days I whispered
to her in bed, in the dark and folded
night, the street-lit glowing elm,

my motorcycle below in the drive.
Those were the days before
I drove into an old woman's windshield.

I have imagined the impact,
the slow-motion spider-webbing of glass,
the barking of a dog in the distance.

I have imagined the necessary things,
my lover in bed beside me,
the silk Arabic her fingers trace

on my stomach, a tree, a sense of danger,
the possible loss of my life.
Instead, helmeted, I caromed after buckling

the glass and only scarred my arm
on the pavement. That's all I know.
I have imagined the woman's white hair

in her shadowed car, the gaze that sees me
through the glass, J.'s eyes as she begins
to come. A life beyond the life I've lived.

LII.

Where a prairie granary's white rigging
is moored below creek-cut hills layered
by autumn's first descant—flaming
maple, sallow larch—two heavy wooded

strands on facing sides begin their blossom
in identical conversions. From the top
their leaves burn in a reverse plume
and the synchronicity of rotated crops.

At night, the granary's light fills this field,
a vacant stadium, as moths and nighthawks
swirl up and up and their chatter tells wild
stories of passion that will not last in awkward

air, in the space of this accumulating night
where angels yearn to touch the earth,
this green world that rises up like light
and falls and fails again. But what worth

might angels have, what song in perfect fifths,
when in the creek bed, chalked with silt,
the salt shale pebbles slowly shift
and in the approaching wind leaves tilt

and weave the air like desire which fades
yet pauses before completion? Once the face
of earth is a damp caress of leaves,
desire vanishes like autumn haze, or grace.

LIII.

My father gazes on a blazing haze, his
Iowa prairies running to the horizon.
The grass is tall and blond and the sun
is going down. My mother joins him,
the dark tears of her hornrims pinching
her face, a squint as if she missed
something in the middle distance.
It is nineteen sixty-three. The world
is changing and they don't even know,
though she will grow her hair long
and he will wear his collars wide.
They are my age and this light
is heavy with unfolding, the dark
opening across the small yellow house
on the cul-de-sac. The day's last light
is long and auburn. It touches their faces
and perhaps I am speaking to them now:
You will have a son and he will love you.
and he will come to love beside a woman
with rain-dark hair.

New days, J. and I cross fields still
golden in the early autumn, watch
the wind pass through this grass

leaving patterns no one ever learns.
You will be happy while you have each other
And the world will change beneath you.

THE COUNTRY OF LOST SONS

(2004)

NARRATIVE

Because it all begins with story,
the telling around the fire tearing
itself free from wood's fingerprint,

the book open on the table beside
a pitcher quivered with Calla lilies
or a fragrant spray of Carolina jasmine

whose honey is said to poison bees,
perhaps I should begin with the U-boat cook
opening his ration box of socks

late in the war. These socks, charcoal,
delicate as shadows in his hands,
made from human hair. He slips

them over his rotten feet and flits
through the ringing narrows, the tunnel
of air he travels with and through.

Or because all narrative is about
the self, personal and florid,
maybe I should begin with the hole

I tore through the ice, star-shaped
and black, the plunge and gasp,
my galvanized saucer swaying beneath me

as the water gave way. I walked home
beneath wind-stripped sycamores,
my clothes frozen into a carapace,

a husk of ice and wind, beneath
which I could shift and move, somehow
preserved from the murderous world.

for Andrew Hudgins

THE COFFEEHOUSE WAR

. . . he will weep much, too late,
when his people are perished from him.

—ILIAD

In the coffeehouse
where I sit in the width
of my day off,

the girl behind the bar
sweeps the counter
into damp circles,

her buckskin hair
curling around her face
like parentheses,

an expression
of continuous afterthought.
The slow pull

of summer runs
deep beside me.
The door opens

in a wave of wet hot air.
There is the weight
of what needs

to be read hanging
above my head:
the giddy heft of Homer,

the triplets of Aeschylus,
and a book by a friend
with its laughing dog cover.

I have hacked
my way into the *Iliad*,
into the rage and sad pain,

into the wet peal
of bronze on bronze,
the squeals of men

who lost their bowels
to the dirt, and hear the echo
of Nestor's censure

of Achilles on the silent TV
that glimmers in the corner.
In Priština, a mob celebrates

the war's end with fireworks—
saffron and gold,
a particularly Cyrillic red—

in an architecture of fire
and smoke beyond
the silhouettes of buildings

pulled down
when the antiaircraft
lashed its dark lettering

across the sky.
Embers filter down
across the town—

this not quite Troy.
And somewhere,
some new Andromache

weeps for her child,
the last to go
over the walls (a postscript

in the closed earth)
beyond which wait
the terrible ships.

NEW POEM

This the point where it begins—
a new story so familiar I hesitate
to start it, sure you'll smile
with that touch of condescension
that says, we've all been *here* before:
the baby boy tearing his bloody way
into the loudbright world,
the father (honestly) sleepy,
the mother soaked with joy.

And how I want the narrative,
the story's arc roping out
like clothesline in a bright wind,
how I want it to function,
like a bridge, the distant shore
leafed out in rutty green, everything
rising out of the rotten dark.

But you know and I know
that's how they all start out—
the everyday light falling over
the transom, chirp and warble
outside the window, a world reborn.
That's how they all start out—
Begin again—elegies I mean.

PARIS

I run through this feud all day
as the sun slides behind tree after tree,
the baroque shadows of day tracing
the curves of my son's sleeping face:
Hector, Patroclus; Achilles, Hector;
Paris, Achilles; Paris—who kills Paris?
That fancy pants dandy. More human
than heroes in his tongue-rich desire.
Does he skate off, no longer necklaced
to his terrifying beauty? Does love's fury
hound him, turned out from the civilized,
some new scar raking his elegant chin?

It's Philoctetes, I learn, the wounded one,
Philoctetes the archer ducking behind
the shields of his aristocratic infantrymen
who planted an arrow to the feathers
in his alabaster side. Paris, amazed
at the iridescent ache of his own blood,
brought somehow out of burning Troy
to expire by the side of Oenone,
the nymph whose bitter love-
lorn heart refused to heal him. My story,
the way I want it, is his to live in:
moving between storm-tossed stones

on a distant shore. I want him
alive for reasons I cannot name. Perhaps,
because I know what becomes of beauty
these days.

PLATO'S EXPULSION

written on an unpaid Chicago parking ticket.

Every poet knows
the story: how Plato
in his tenth book

turned the poets out
of his *Republic*.
Plato's art

worked like the backs
of men striped
with sweat,

laboring with marble,
or women turning
furrows in earth

with small hoes.
It was the gates
of Hades

not Achilles' shield,
the artless emblem
negated in precise

abstraction.
His gates close
on a night lost

in floating
leaves lit spinning
in the streetlight,

a cupped hand
bent in touching,
the trills of a woman

whistling Bach,
long, whiskey-
colored light

cut to stripes
on a gray cell
wall, fat piles

of shit
smoldering
in the corner.

Ten thousand burning
trees, a wing,
this unflinching expulsion.

THE PLANE DESCENDING

The plane descending
                through the sky's collapse,
through an indigo
          lightshow,
              split-fingered
lightning
       painting the clouds'
              colonnade,
the way the wing lights
            beat
              against the dark,
small, too small,
        cabin pressure
             holding steady.
I (always that lyric *I*—
        inventing
            and pretending—
a fly vivacious
       between
            the window and the screen)
I want you
      to see this as fear,
          I want
to make you feel
        that snap at the ribs
             as the plane

drops
        to catch on the next swell
                      of air,
the glue
      inside your mouth
               as the lightning
rivets the purple sky.
               But such gesture
                       is foolish—
you are comfortable
          where you are,
                reading this,
the soft lights
        and the good chair,
              late Beethoven,
perhaps,
      on the stereo.
             Or the comfortable jostle
of the train
      as it clatters
          down the trestle
toward the river
      and the tunnel,
          a skyline
full of light
      rising up behind you.

HECTOR IN HELL

It is Hector who lingers near
the wall, the stone bright
under the ten-year sun. He waits
when Andromache has turned
her back on him to raise
dirges for a man not yet dead
within the walls of Troy,
when his son has been taken
from him. He waits there
before Paris rousts him.
He waits there and must hold
the moment carefully:
his son's screams
at the horse-hair plume,
the bronze-ridged eyes
turned to a bubble of laughter
as he is tossed in the air.
The helmet set aside
on the cracked path.
Andromache watching
with shining eyes. He crosses
the threshold and stands now
in the lens of the story,
the noon sun targeting him
with his shadow, but in
the black thickets of Hades,
he will gently lift his son again
and be lifted with him.

TEMPTATION

Weep not just yet: for you must later weep
For wounds inflicted by another sword.
—CANTO 30

She has unwrapped the gates of hell,
but he wants her eyes like firelight
across the room, slow days in bed,
striped light across the sheets,
a braid of legs beneath. He wants
to dress her in the moonlight and
the exquisite twinge of her departure,
the skin behind her knee. He wants
the pleasure of her baking bread
in a stone-floored kitchen, deer
nuzzling the azalea buds beyond
the window. Dark rivers crossed
by white bridges. The undisturbed
air above their son's sleeping head.

But, when Beatrice first appears
in the garden high in Purgatory,
rafted down on angels' wings
and clothed in weeping flame,
Dante cannot meet her eyes.
He drops his gaze upon the Lethe—
dark and mirrored as the unforgiven
desire of Paolo and Francesca.

His reflection shames him once again.
In te, Domine, speravi—the words
of the psalm hauled up into the trees
by the angelic chorus. *Do you not know,*
she asks him, *that man is* happy *here?*

THE COUNTRY OF LOST SONS

In the ninth month of my son's life
I begin to dream of him
crushed beneath the wheels
of a fat panel van. In the quick

breath of terror that follows,
I know (*somehow*, in the *donnée*
of dreams) that he is not dead.
Is miraculously uninjured,

and the dream slips into
a caravan of lost worlds
and carnival gestures as I race
(purposelessly now) towards

the beckoning emergency room.
What is startling, as I wake,
is the ease with which I am pushed
from the velvet edge of this dream—

the horror that is equaled only
in its perfect clarity by the absolute,
gutty elation of his continuing breath,
the warm pucker of his soft mouth

I find, slipping out of bed and down
the moon-speckled hall to check

again each night. Later that week,
an early evening tinged with indigo,

the perfume of a thousand rhododendrons
flashing against the dark, wide shine
of the Willamette, listening to an old friend
read from his new book, I hear

the words beyond the words,
the ragged blue-black edge to all this
easy, forgiving grief: *my son
is my elegy, waiting to be written.*

for Sherod Santos

AGAINST PROGNOSTICATION

I have not written about my son's future,
not yet. How he will read and reread

the *Audubon Field Guide* and memorize each bird,
how he will wander off under dappled light

and return home in a squad car. Not because
I can't imagine the way he will carefully

hold his hand above his heart after he has unfurled
the skin from his meaty thumb, or how he will rip apart

a frog hind legs to jaw and how he will feel after.
I have not talked about the day he will wrap

his friend's car around a tree and *somehow*
walk away, leaving the scene limping

home to sleep in bloody sheets.
Not out of fear, though this genealogy hints at it.

This reticence is caution not reprimand—
what can he learn, anyway, from such a history?

That day will still come when he opens his palm
above a flame and smells himself burning.

Perhaps, by then his father will be brave enough
to let him have his own life, but I will not say,

be comforted, for comfort comes at a price.
And I will not talk about what comes next:

a girl, a kiss, a field of grass. His thin heart
tearing as she leaves. That part of the story

is all anyone wants, denouement
and then the singing, operatic camerawork

pulling back to reveal his loneliness in the grass,
blue herons stalking through a salt marsh at sunset,

ten glaucous gulls and a black back on the gables
of the paintworks riding out the storm

UNTITLED

Sunlight reflected
         off the puddle
                on the slate
back steps,
      the remains
          of a late rain
on stone I laid
        by hand
           (the wet saw
that cut each to fit
         left its grit
in the basin
       like waste spun
           in a gold pan),
that light hits the ceiling
        and the last drops
from the hawthorn
      or the gutters
           full
and overflowing
      cast ripples
         on the ceiling
as if the floor's invisible
       and in the bedroom
            now
the rain keeps falling.

There's no message here,
no one's dead,
my wife and I
aren't splitting up,
the weather isn't reading us
better than
we read ourselves.
If she were here,
I might call to her
and lead her
up the stairs
to lay down
in the clean light,
the trees ticking
around us
like a collection of clocks,
but
she's at work and I'm alone,
and how this turns
to story I can't say.
The slate means little
more than effort
and pride
and the light means
less than that.
The rain has stopped
and you're on your own.
The careful drip
of meaning
falls on the act
of making and unmaking
alike,

as flocks of starlings

                      flecked with gold

wash around

              a tree-soaked sky.

TERRIBLE GESTURES

It has happened again.
As the planes slammed
into the silver towers
and the smoke wept out
like solder bannered
in the wind, as the steel
got weak in the knees,
a man and a woman—
strangers, lovers, perhaps
friends, does it matter?—
came together in the torn
burning, in the trembling
and clamor of glass.
They held hands, each
small comfort to the other,
and stepped into the air.
They held hands
as they fell, a gesture
that leaves me no peace.
It has happened again,
this terrible blessing of hope.

GOODNIGHT NOBODY

The late afternoon light settles down around them on the bed and my son stills—the first time all day. He is on his back on the bed, *Goodnight Moon* beside his head. My wife's voice articulate as sapphire in the air among the swoops of dust and light:

> *And a comb and a brush*
> *and a bowl full of mush*
> *And a quiet old lady*
> *who was whispering hush.*

Outside this room, the world is all Kosovo. Mass graves and the arms of children in the rubble. In Lastica, the radio correspondent reports, Serbian militias were looking for one special girl. The town beauty. Unable to get their hands on her, "They took a 13-year-old instead," remarks NPR.

It's the *instead* that gets me, really, the marking off of one life for another, that child taken and torn into beneath the wound-blue moon of her eye. The lucky one (with her "striking green eyes and black hair") squirreled away in borrowed, ratty clothes, hidden among a surprising weight of women. She survives to tell her story across the border in Macedonia. All the women gather together again.

The other one is hiding from us now, from all of us, an innuendo, an accusation fading back between the towers of sycamore, following the edges of the billowing hillsides. She waits in the wet grass that slaps at her broken feet, hoping to come home, but the *hiss* of that terrible word gives her up instead, its echo lingering in the voice on my radio.

II.

Out walking the dogs, I pass a boy, seven or eight years old, who takes aim with a broomstick at a single engine Bellanca flying low. The sound of the plane taut in the sky. It dips its wings and turns into the wind to make the approach to the airport beyond the rim of elms that ring our park. The boy is enraptured. He aims with a broom and spits out the sound of automatic weapon fire between his swollen lips, following the plane's trajectory across the sky. The plane falls away toward the runway as if this small boy has actually shot it down.

III.

My son is eleven months old and as I sit with him the television is on: CNN broadcasting from Kosovo. The image is antiaircraft above Priština. Shadowy crowds moving beneath the casement of the lens. Fires snapping in the streets.

Julian turns to the TV only when the commercials break in and, even then, only when there's music. When the

Burger King cheeseburger soundtrack strikes up the *William Tell Overture* he turns to the set on his hands and knees and shakes like a dog with joy.

IV.

When the sunlight piles into our bedroom in the late afternoon, full of dust, Julian reaches for it and wants, I think, to taste it. And when his hand come away empty, he'll try again. Sitting cinematically among his stacking blocks, he reaches for the black strap of the camera I am using to try and hold this moment. He pushes towards me. I put him back. He pushes towards me again and again I put him back, and suddenly my son turns away from me, his voice, rising and assembling itself in the air around him. It fills the small room, the lunatic sound of his anger. That anger that gives his life its life, a sudden white urgency among the chattering colors

Is this it? How we come to know that we know? The self suddenly beside the self, turned spectator in the theater of loss and anger.

V.

He is trying to stand on his own. In the middle of the room on the soft rug, he'll stand up, wobble, and fall back on his butt. Then he'll do it again. Ten, twenty times. It's like watching an elephant learn to jump.

The caterpillars in Annie Dillard's *Pilgrim at Tinker Creek* march endlessly around the rim of a potted plant, each following chemical markers laid down by the one just ahead. Seven days. Straight. Pure will. That's Julian. Stand. Wobble. Fall. Stand. Wobble. Fall. His shock of blond hair doing its Andy Warhol thing. My caterpillar of a child.

VI.

They have found a boy again in the weeds near Ohio, where the trains slow and clatter over the rails, the ties sounding out the rhythm of a dirge. I don't want to bring this in now, but the boy had his genitals cut off. Oh God, I don't want to say this. His trunk sliced to stripes of flesh, and the mottled glimpse of bone, his flesh turned the color of the swooping puzzle of the overpass. I don't want to make a bed of grief, to lie down in it again each night, but I have a son, and it is all I can do to hold him still beneath the ruined starlight.

VII.

There are three of them playing in the sand. My son, a girl a year or so his elder, and her brother pushing at the fences of two. The day is high and bright—fall careening down through the perfect density of blue. The girl's hair glissades as Julian tackles her. They laugh, splayed like fingers in the sand. The two-year old doesn't understand the game and begins to scream. An intoxicating, wordless scream that goes on and on. Ten minutes pass and he will not be calmed, his face an umber work.

We finally separate them and move to go, pulling on our shoes and socks, the day falling beyond the shadow-sketching hills. The boy's mother brings him over to apologize, his *sorry* small and wet and barely healed. Julian leans in and with his tiny fist punches him, hard.

VIII.

Now I am reading to my son with the remains of a rain still ticking off the fat catalpa leaves. My arms around him, the book before him on his knees.

Goodnight comb
And goodnight brush
Goodnight nobody
Goodnight mush.

Goodnight to the old lady
whispering hush.

Outside the window, beyond my son's quiet form, a road sign flashes in the blond grass, the vacant lot clumped with the rubble of old cars, a school bus up on blocks. Outside the window, the muted hills are torn with lines of the fall wheat-harvest, dust and fallow, the sky chalked with gray. Outside the window, the air is rich, the color of claret. Outside the window, my son . . . *hush*, I think . . . the weight of his life above him like moons, like stones.

HE ARRANGES HIS POEMS

on the floor,
        the grid of a dig,
                Pelmanism,
stonework,
        architecture of want.
                    Outside,
wind spindles
        among bare branches,
windows
        spiked with frost.
                Black cherries
in a glass of syrah.
           Sweaty leather.
                Pepper.
Books snigger
        from their shelves.
                Early dark
trundles down around them.
              He could
sit there all night
        and nothing
                would be made clear,
except the bruised globe
           of the wine.
And what good
        would it do
           to rail

against the arched
                and cautious world,
the world
       so stingy
           with its gifts
that weather
       becomes
           a kind of miracle?
The weather.
       Honestly,
           he doesn't even know
what to ask for
       anymore.
The wind rises
       or dies
           in the weltering cold.
Leaves tick
       along the pavement
              like clocks.
Snow begins to fall.
       Or not.
           It all depends
on the arrangement.

YORK HARBOR

Dragons live forever
Not so little boys . . .

If there are dragons in the world, they lie
down on the body of the river like fog.
Their bodies froth in the cold morning air,
the rising sun tearing at their wings
as boats clutch at each other in the harbor.
My son has dreamed badly and climbs into
my bed in the fragile cabin we share.
The light up early over the ocean. Stone
and water. *A dragon was eating my hair*,
he whimpers. I hush him, but everything
I would do to keep the wind from the door
is doomed. He turns back to sleep, stretching
his long legs into the warmth I've made.
I know this now: I will lose my son and
I will find him. No morning will equal
this morning and many will, many will.

RENOVATION

(2005)

TELEVISION IN ANOTHER LANGUAGE

Through the blue swale
of the room's small black and white,
a woman, in what must be red taffeta,

pauses in seduction—her husband's lawyer—
her breath on his neck from beneath
a veil of blond lace. There's more than this,

a fading caress; such scenes come to nothing,
blank as the emerald arch-lit hallway
which empties into the Place Nationale,

the dark shadows of cannons, shuffling
pigeons and beyond, the stairs descending
from the alley's dark cobbles

into some other tongue, gestures which slip
inside the star-dark constellation in the mirror
of a bar lined with corked bottles luminous

with pickled fish, octopus and squid,
a mirror that gives back the smoke
of a room where words choke the air,

languages in whorls above the cracked plaster,
dusted bricks, books, half-opened bottles of wine.
Remember the sunlit, glass-bricked girders,

the loaves of black bread and duck canvas counters
of the Marché St. Émelion layered with iced pike
and albacore, dripping water slipping into the sewers?

But this is Lisbon—the bar's slick tile
littered with whole fried fish, small as fingers
on greased paper plates. Behind us

in the mirror, men crowd tables to mutter
over Portugal's loss to Brazil, their talk
as old as the smoke-soaked stones.

There is a language for all this. Consonant
and vowel. Sunlight through glass, black girders.
Football under blaring halogen. Fish bathed

in cracked ice. Begin again . . . There is a red dress.

THE AVENUE OF CHANCE ASCENT

I.

Below the rows of towering live oaks,
  Barcelona's hash hustlers pass through
newspaper shacks and the lilt of gelato vendors
  and Las Ramblas descends to the sparkle

of the polluted Costa Brava where it splits
  like genealogy, but if you leave the trees
and walk past the flames that lick the racks
  of roasting chickens and the heavy metal

cowboys who will have, just before you pass,
  crashed the jewelry shop's plate glass
and scattered with diamonds and silver
  and handfuls of tinsel, you might see

in these streets bending back and again
  a darkness, a shadow which gathers as sound
below the window: the cough of bus exhaust,
  the rattle of bottles delivered to Cafe Romano,

the maid running her vacuum through
  frayed hallways and the disinterested lobby,
the chortle of doves on the balcony
  of a room where I'm curled in damp sleep,

trying to wash away the vodka I had hoped
   would ease me into the night train's sway.
I couldn't sleep in the Pyrenees,
   outside of Andorra, the side rail held a wreck

of railcars, where the pull of explosives
   had opened and rolled the metal back into
a corolla of black petals. I watched the dark hills
   roll into the exploding dawn, into today

where I've broken open the morning, stepping
   from a train of Paris' disregard
into Catalan's breath, husky as tar, where,
   through it's not even ten, in the plaza

drunks in high zeal whirl with fireworks
   to celebrate Spring; *Festival du Printemps*
says the desk's frail man in broken French—
   our accident of a common language—

as his hands hook in his vest and he winces
   with every explosion.

II.

Awake in the afternoon, echoing fireworks
  startle, again and again, the rock doves
who whirl in continuous curves round
  the dry fountain. Yet, it's a calm one,

I'm told. The year before, hogs ran wild
  through the quarter; a tractor trailer
on the slaughterhouse run rolled the tight turn
  around the *Mirador de Colón*. Streets thick

with frenzied pigs and smoking steel,
  a dazed woman amazed her husband died
so easily, her blue dress charred and open
  at the throat, a gray hand dappled

with ash that says: accident or not,
  it's the crash, the act of exploding
and every evolving opening, death's million
  possible doors which define us.

High above water, where the streets fill
  with Carnival, I hook a woman's arm
and we shout open bottles of dollar champagne
  and serpentine through penny games,

fathers with sharp tongues, the glitter
  and snatches of Spanish; the street smells
of sausage and garlic and wine; my hand
  on her neck, slender beneath

the dark savanna of her hair
  and the water of her eyes
which sparkles as fireworks thud above,
  all feathers and tufts of crimson and gold—

our ancient need to praise the rise
  of winter's survivors and consecrate
the surge of Spring that expands
  and explodes as surely as it dies,

leaving only this dark vacancy
  of sky we rush again to fill.

RENOVATION

I. THE OLD CITY, PRAGUE, 1990

Here the astronomical clock
off *Staromestske Namesti*
persists its intricate swirls
of hour and moon, the fragile circle
spun within the larger face
like a drafter's template:
Charles the First blinded
its architect so he could
never build another.

And here in '68, Jan Palach
set himself ablaze. Sloshing petrol
he knelt, and with the catch
of the match, folded, burning.

And how he must have walked,
daily, blindly remembering how
his clock balanced—one odd window
off to the left—how the numerals
in gold leaf glowed when the sun
rose and fell with little warmth
on a woman, scarfed and creased,
selling bundles of potatoes,
small yellow apples.

He would never see
the followers of Jan Hus
throng through the streets
raising fervent dust. Or see
them broken like joists
under the Catholic purge.

When the smoke rose
across Hus and his sweat ran
thick as wax, an old woman
tossed her bundle on the pyre.
"Sanctas simplicatas," was all he said.

Here above the rise of Victorian balconies,
concrete planters line Wenceslas Square,
circles of bare dirt and the walls of one
are coated with wax, a thick ochre-blue
spreading downhill.
                    When again,
late in 1989, people rose from their cellars,
their faces the color of gritty stone,
they planted candles by the thousand:
a ring of light splattering their dancing,
their flags of celebration. Smoke rose
and wax ran like rain.

There's a monument moored
in the square, large, sudden
and ominous. Slick black stone
wraps Hus as his followers raise
their fists in defiance and failure.

Palach's shrine is pine plastered
with wax and dead petals,
a mark on the wall.
                    And here,
near the National, where young men
queue to haggle for western cash,
a woman, her eyes dark as char,
wants to sell me peppers, wants
to sell me apples, potatoes,
wants to sell me anything.

II. ELEGY, 1953

Say this: the bridge bent to touch
the glossy Monongahela. Or say,
the bridge collapsed like ribs
puckering the dark lungs of water.

It is in every way the same.

There was a bridge over a river.
Red granite scarred with quartz,
old with smoke from the barges
that year round furrowed the water

and, just above flood stage, houses
circled the valley: fading, fretworked gables
and the slouch of small barns.

A cracked plaster kitchen, his two hands
around a coffee mug. Her pinched look.
A silver radio on the refrigerator
as outside, in the shadows, the water rose.

III. FERMATA: MADISON, WISCONSIN

A dark Indian runner stripes the oak
risers of the stairs, and photos ascend

in brass frames, fading yellow to gray.
A stereo still plays on wooden crates of albums.

A boy slack in a chair. Sycamore and sugar maple.
This town is the same. I could have been gone

a summer. I've been gone seven years.
The comma between *Please* and *Stop*

holds this world suspended. Still,
I would reach to this boy, then seventeen,

take his hands from the stock of that .30-06.
I would say: This is what you have given me,

I have placed cups of orchids on the water.
I would say, *The silence of God is God.*

Please, stop.

There must be a way—every language
has a word for soul and, in nearly every one,

it's the sound of breath leaving the body.

IV. THE NIGHT OF THE BARRICADES, PARIS, 1968

In the yellow light of rue Gay Lussac
students muster, thousands
sprawling through the breathless streets,

blocked from the Seine and the Sorbonne
by ranks of black masks, truncheons, dogs.

They dig into the Quartier Latin: heaped cobbles
and beneath, buried yellow sand.

The barricades multiply—bricks and billboards,
scaffolding, signposts, cars. Veins of smoke lace
through the air. The wet rage of Molotov cocktails.

Dark shells, cars, flipped and burnt,
appear along the smoking morning streets.
Shattered glass, a rubble of stone.

In a flower shop off Montparnasse
a woman sweeps glass from the shelves.
In the broken window, her sunflowers
hunch, touched by the ashen light.

For long months graffiti will appear in the night:

Allons-y!
Soyons Cruel!
Courion, le vieux monde est en arrière.

Run, the old world is behind you.

V. RENOVATION, BERLIN, 1990

Tonight, Roger Waters will perform *The Wall*
on Potsdamer Platz, before the ruined shadows
      of the Kaiser Wilhem cathedral

where Unter den Linden ends in a dust-baked field,
ends in scaffolding—
they are renovating history.
                    The Brandenburg Gate
in the wind, an arched trellis of rippling cloth.

1944: two soldiers hunker in the cathedral.
Concussions in the distance. The faint
patter of rainwater on the altar.

Tables of Russian officers' hats, olive felt, red satin,
infantry medals pinned on a sash.

Scrap flakes of painted cement.
Hammers and chisels for rent by the hour.

They take quarter-hour sightings through the ash-wet air
and report in over the radio:

    All's clear. Clear. Clear.

Hammer's ring across the platz. Cement dust frosts
our arms. We carry pieces of the Wall in cupped hands.

Beneath the crowd, a killing ground,
where soldiers once cut racing backs with crosshairs.

Drinking rain from tin cups, they talk of the bodies
they find, rarely those left behind.

Towards midnight, helicopters chop the summer air,
and above the tattered stars.
                              When the show's over
we've been in the dirt for hours.

—for Crow

VI. AUTUMN AND SPRING: MADISON, WISCONSIN

ai ai legoi!

We passed the ember of a joint
on the breakwater early nights in fall;
our faces occasionally amber
in the air sharp with coming snow.

Flickering on the water, lights rose
above the dark, rock jetty.

Your words, coughed out in smoke,
billowed in the haloed lights
and now you hang before me,
a rasping ghost, a thought,
if I had listened when you said:
I will take my life. But those aren't
your words; they're mine.
I have given them to you in the silence.

Lake Winona still frozen, we stepped
down off the dock, into the fog,
the lights, an early night in early Spring:
the last damp snow and small puddles
on the ice. Out far enough,
the world goes white. In a year

you'll be dead. All that reaches us
is the crack and echoing boom
of the ice breaking up out in deep water.

The smaller lake, Verona, cattails and
redwings, the air is warming but the water
is cold. Nothing comes from nothing.
Patterned grass washed in the wind
doesn't mean you're dead, nor
the white-tail crushed against dark lindens
on the Arboretum drive. Pine needles
desiccate and fall in circles of bronze,
the hyacinth, stamped with sorrow,
I placed upon the water.

VII. THE ASSASSINATION OF LUIS DONALDO COLOSIO, 1994

CNN runs again and again this footage of the pistol,
        the hand rising from the crowd,
the bloody flap of skull.

Again and again, the hand rising in the smeared crowd,
        again the wisp of smoke.
Circled accomplices shoulder security
        aside. A voice crying:

    I have saved Mexico.

The hand rises again. The body never falls.

VIII. THEFT ELEGY: ST. LOUIS, MISSOURI

A later friend and I drank late
that night, the dying time

of spring, before August sears the air
and in the city there is no sanctuary

but the width of starless nights.
Cars slick in the streetlights

and from a blossoming pear a mockingbird
sounded snatches of waxwing,

the cardinal's soft diphthong.
Oriel-call and birdsong beyond name

came from a space beyond flowers,
from the dark heart of that tree,

luxurious, liquid. A street emptied
by the hour and in your room

at the top of the stairs, light
suddenly blazed, blossomed

across the limestone sills. The secret
of that light fell in ashes on the grass.

IX. ENVOI

In the photo, it is far from certain, but
perhaps, after weeks of rain, the hills slid

into the monastery outside of Andorra—
the church steps buried nave-deep,

vespers in a silent street—all we can say
is that he has bared his head,

cowl on his shoulders, as he kicks through streets
usually filled with sausage vendors wreathed in steam

and the glassman's rapping call echoing
off the flagstones. The dark-haired daughter

of the butcher who flirts with men around
the fountain. This is not a world

at war. This world is suddenly fluid
and a girl at the Café Mallorca sipping

from a bowl of chocolate invites herself
into the poem. She looks toward us,

a black smear of wet hair across her cheek.
Her skin smells of anise and as he passes

their eyes meet. Yet what we might imagine
is the moment before the moment

of the photo, the moment of opening the door
from the flickering cloister, his shoulder

against oak, the smell of varnish and wax,
candle smoke, wool. He throws his slender frame

against the door and the earth moves a little,
the mud against the door which he barely slips through.

IMAGINARY NUMBERS

$$i^2 = {}^.1$$

As in light coming distances
in the humming blankness
from stars already shuttered
and collapsed, as in the volume
of water not in a bottle, the area
of the shadow of a missing limb.
The way winter light through
glass warms nothing. The speed
at which, on the rain-slick
leaf-scattered Kittaning Pike,
the accident doesn't happen,
the car doesn't slew and swing
out against the oncoming traffic,
the horns don't blare, glass
doesn't turn to a geometry
of pain and so she returns home
after work with dusk
already clambering up the house,
the porch light out, haphazard
mail and the message light
flashing down the hall.

It could be that her child,
gone to stay with his father,
has called to say he loves her,

or that her husband has left her
for another man, a rodeo clown,
and she won't know whether
to be enraged or amused.
Or perhaps it's her dentist
confirming her appointment
as her cats twine between
her legs, demanding to be fed.

If possibility is the square
of experience, what can she say
of this day, its unknown grief
haunting the house, painting
the walls with its brushwork
of headlight and shadow? Would
she wish to take it to the root,
the absolute *i* on the margins
of a tertiary world? Outside,
the rain begins again and
slaps the grass, the trees'
bare limbs scaffolding
the exponential dark.
She snaps on the light
and sees herself repeated
in the mirror, at once doubled
and inexplicably exhausted.

FUCKING ON THE CONFEDERATE DEAD

Shall we take the act

To the grave?

—ALLEN TATE

Summer is the adulation of the moon
on her bare breasts, his mouth on the moon,
her hand on his chest with the grass cold
and wet beneath them. The brute curiosity
of her hair curtains off his face, though
tonight the headstones are tables overflowing
with everything their separate pasts desire,
the fragrance of it on the air—wet roses,
ashes, oil—as deer hop the wall and ghost
around the stones in earshot of the soft Morse
of secret pleasure. Headlights bare above
their bodies the trees and stones
dissolving day by day and he enters
her white flesh, enters a meadow of sighs.

You hear the shout, the crazy hemlocks point,
the rocks relax somewhat of their hardness.
The oaks lean in and willows circle us all
within the green effervescence of their hair.

"Who was it you called for?"
Her reply before she kisses him again
is world weary, a tenuous grace note—
Oh, it's a long story. One you've heard before.

No time now for that last story, no time
for Orpheus and the croaking dactyls
of his unremitting grief. And, honestly,
what could he say to ease your mind?
Such narratives demand renovation, so
turn your eyes from the immodest present
and all the bodies exhausting each other
on the rain-wet grass, the melting stones.
Leave the suspiration of the earth, the chuffing deer.
Gather together in the dark hours. Start now.

BIRDWATCHING IN WARTIME

(2009)

LANDSCAPE WITH SWELLING
AND HIVES

And here, or there . . . No. Should we have stayed at home,

wherever that may be?

—ELIZABETH BISHOP

When the *tsawaim* swam from the deadfall across the path
      (a moss-grown nurse log
hosting a thrumming mess of life in its rain-woven campus),
      when those wasps
stapled my back and sides and face and sent me at a run down
      the piebald path,
when the rainforest trembled, fishtail palms kicking their fins
      in the green welter
beneath the canopy, when the splotches flushed across my arms,
      my neck, my sweat-licked face,
when the diaspora of venom wrote a question across my back
      in hot letters that left me
cold and shaking and desperately needing to piss, I had no sense,
      stunned and numb,
that my throat might close, not even when my tongue went dumb
      like a river
fat with flood, no thought that the last sight I'd see would be
      a green shriek
of light carried through the trees. The wasps stung for nothing
      I had done;
the others passed that path before me. The chill washed out
      in sweat,

and the landscape tumbled back to form, but, hours out,
        perhaps
I should have made my peace, prepared myself among the *pitchurina*
        and *pucahuasca*
and waited for the infinite to break through the canopy in a spray
        of green-gone-gold.
In the end, nothing came of this. My throat stayed open and
        the canopy closed.
It's the distance out from camp—the gas lamps lit and tented
        in the shifting dark,
the house macaw patrolling the piered walkways, little chevrons
        flashing on his shoulders—
that makes it menacing. Yes, it would have been a pity not to have seen
        the spattered sun
scribbled down to nothing more than matchlight on army ants
        engraving leaf litter,
the cuneiform of tapir prints in the mud of that flat-banked stream,
        not to have seen
the wattled jacana scrawl across water lilies with her vast, forked feet,
        a pity
never to have taken piranha from the river and watched them slap
        their gibberish
across the bottom of the boat, yes, a pity never to have read the remains
        of a saddleback tamarin
(a slur of fur and black fingers) as the fact of a jaguar in the night,
        yes, a pity, yes,
but what now's the answer to that question written across my skin?

LANDSCAPE WITH FLOODED FOREST

Amazonia, January 2004

I.

When the horizon rises up around the shoulders of the trees
and fish fly through branches in flocks of scale

and saucer eyes, and the bird-hunters billboard webs
across the water in the shrubby canopy

of ceiba and cercropia, the strangler fig splayed out
in a skeletal fan and colonnades of kapok,

when the white sun soon finishes off the dawn
and tree boas sleep tentacled above the water

across a fan of leaves to avoid the crush of noon,

II.

when a wire-tailed manakin flames
through the middle-story treetops and pink dolphins

slalom through the sunken trunks
to hunt tambaqui that feed on fallen fruit,

tiny coconuts of summer's plenty,

when the seeping tannin water, deep as steeped tea,
consumes the edges of the trees

and we float above a forest doubled in the water
(a clicking symphony of fish trickles

up through our wooden canoe),

the water will be halfway up the sky
and not yet finished rising.

III.

At night, beneath ficus trunks that arch and plunge
in gothic tangles, the bang and stammer

of the tree frogs' need orchestrates desire in the forest.
Quarter-sized they come gluey off the mimosa,

eyes red as blood blisters

beneath our lights, as the golden foil of caiman eyeshine
along the banks balances

IV.

the smear of stars across the sky.

V.

Tarantulas that hunt fish—the black goliath and the Peruvian
pinktoe—strike out across the water as we pass

and a blue-crowned trogan

sits stunned and blinking beneath our headlamps.

We raise the landscape into meaning and return it

damaged in our wake—the slap

of water off the paddles, the sweep and beam of lights
tunneling through the dark.

Trauma is what we carry and the world retires from us
in radiating waves, but (*recall it now!*)

VI.

the frogs, they deafened us that night.

VII.

Horned screamers play a quartet across the high-ground
grass, as we haul our canoe through the canopy

branch by branch

like boat-building simians. This ancient bird
we're searching for, the hoatzin,

in the wet savannah remnants, croaks and heaves—
a heavy smoker's wheeze—

VIII.

beneath the deadwood overhead, a blue-faced, mohawked relic
(a claw-winged, almost *archaeopteryx*).

It lizard-hops and pants trying to stay cool. We eat and wait
and watch the heat pile clouds up the sky.

Rain threatens its black opera as we slip out
through the trees writing down birds for inscrutable lists.

IX.

Anis and oropendulas crisscross the open canopy
where three rivers seam together, kingfishers

chatter, skimming low and loud above the russet water,

and at our feet jerk piranha, red-bellied as rage.
Morpho butterflies spatter the streaked light sapphire.

Soaked with birdcall and blue fluttering, the trees
fill with water and the swift kick of fins.

The air charged with all that hasn't happened yet,
the water with all that has—

X.

the toucan that will be taken from a branch and guzzled
to bloody feathers and the hard beak tip

by a harpy eagle.
Piranhas that disassembled a swimming sloth.

Lakes drain out of the basin leaving a shoreline scoured.
Banks reappear in a maze of mud.

The season of want approaches and recedes. The sunlight
and the heat, and, soon,

the water giving way.

BIRDWATCHING IN WARTIME

The rain comes and the sound
of water hitting water raises
an ovation, the canal pocky
with applause. We move up river,
hoods up, heads down, the boat
ottering through the trees. When
sunlight breaks free and disrobes
in the canopy, we see the heron—
a tiger—striped and striated
and thick on a snag. She rolls
her shoulders, wings out to catch
the light, rainforest backlit
behind her, looming up like praise.

At sunset, a *guanacaste*, a single
sculpted cone of flooded forest
rising from water licked with
the last light, currents of lavender
and ginger drawing through
the slough, water and a tree,
solitary. Then a multitude
of birds, flamingo gawky but
a deeper red, come dropping in
along the water to rise and cup
the wind and awkward fall into
branches against a failing sky.

All night, scarlet ibis paint
that tree, drop by unbearable drop.

In the early dawn, a trogon stoic
as a general in the ficus and great
green macaws in the crowns
of wild almonds—metallic calls,
little soldiers with their chevroned
shoulders. They storm through
the canopy raining almond shells
like shrapnel on the forest floor.
Dawn marshals above the trees
as the light assembles on their tops,
marches down the canopy. How
easily it turns, how quickly words
slip, like knives into rinds. My hushed
footsteps through leaflitter,
my DEET-numb lips. The guides
have left us, sick from metaphor,
scopes up on their shoulders
like rifles. They have long since felt
a change in the weather and step
awkwardly away through shin-deep
mud and fishtail palms, calling
after toucans: *Dios-te-dé, Dios-te-dé!*
In their minds they are already laughing
and smoking beneath the lean-to
as the rain gallops down around them.

TWIN

Fall has finally come in a torrent
that tears leaves from the locust—
glitter mucking up the gutter,
choking the storm sewer, water
backing up, bowed with oil and filmy—
and, no, what it makes me think of
is not love dying, the glorious bronze
rage and ruin of the last days, and
not my own age yammering in the dark
as it loses control of its bladder again
and the piss rains golden as shame
on the mat before the toilet, no,
not all that, but strangely enough,
a cat, a particular cat locked in a box,
forced to live its life stalking corners,
unaware of the isotope's decay hanging
fire in that space like a bare bulb,
the one that will split its life in two (two
halves unhalved and parallel): one cautious,
alive and aware, green foil of eyeshine,
the other flat and black as a burn
on the floor. They exist together,
the carcass and the stalking silhouette,

witched together by possibility's spell.
But I'm afraid it's all just metaphor,
quantum reflection in the mirror of desire.
Not the cat alive *or* dead, but both
at once: love and its failure, metaphor
and madness, youth and age with
its orchestra of sighs, the leaves
streaming through the storm-rich dark
and the mess they cause in the gutter.
Metaphor strokes the cat and buries it,
slides out from beneath the last daylight,
straightens her skirt and smoothes her
pink-streaked hair. Metaphor turns the air
to viognier and buys a round for the house—
she's generous that way. Metaphor
fucks a guy she finds in the bathroom,
makes him a poet. Metaphor stalks
through the night, painting the air
with a waste of _____ that makes even
bridges beautiful. She wakes in the morning
without regret, but Metaphor doesn't talk
about her twin brother, locked away
in the hospital, pacing an ellipse
into the carpet beneath the single bulb
always on in that windowless room.

AMERICAN PASTORAL

First, there's the rank stupidity
of their mucilaginous mouths,
their wide rolling eyes

that look up as you pass (your dog
at your heels) like white Jell-O
molds bouncing on a bumped table

where the burgers and hot dogs
line up eager as children
before the condiments and cheese,

flaccid sheaves of iceberg lettuce,
and the watermelon smiles
echo the cisterns of bunting

that hang from the slatted porch
in the sunlight. Chewy automatons,
but there's a sentimentality to the way

they spread themselves across
the field, the shattered yin-yang
of their hides, the way they clump

together beneath the thin, stripped
maples, their square butts ripe
with flies. The fields flow over

the hill and beyond, the blue sky
speckled with the white froth
of the clouds and the cows

plotz and shuffle their thickness
down to the farmer who has moved
across this field on his quad-runner,

the fenders flared and startled
with mud, and it is no longer
the century you were imagining.

The farmer has his laptop out
and enters a herd of data
into the machine, driving it

through his Wi-Fi to the small barn
of a spreadsheet, taming it the way
his cows are tame, microchip ear-tags
dangling like the last leaves in autumn.

LANDSCAPE WITH URBAN ELEPHANTS

No one knows exactly how many elephants there are in Bangkok.
—PBS

Up from the dumps and the red hollows
where water wells from the bottle-speckled mud,

up from the scrub and cracked palms, up from the can-fires
into the dazzle and slither of traffic muscling

around these boulders of hide and waddle,
up from a distant bliss of tree fern and orchid,

from mahogany and kapok, the elephants come
to the city. Big-shouldered and wattled.

Their slow bop strut up the boulevards,
a repertoire of rolled eights kept by the metronome

of bottlebrush tails syncopated by reflecting tape
patched across their asses. Painting elephants,

dancing elephants, peanut-eating, banana-slinging
elephants, half-smiles and great, gray Walt Whitman eyes

above the bike lights that swing from their trunks.
Traffic swerves around their oil-slick piles of shit.

Beneath it all, a squall of noise, flutter of trunks,
they sing: platter-foot, big toe, skin of wet burlap.

They sing: It don't mean a thing if it ain't got that swing.
Deep into the night alight with sodium

their back-beat rumbles travel for miles, pacing
a high-hat rhythm the tuk-tuks keep beneath the Skytrain.

They totter off to sleep it off beneath the milk-colored
dawn as their tails keep their own rough time.

CELESTIAL EMPORIUM OF
BENEVOLENT KNOWLEDGE:
A SEQUENCE

In "The Analytical Language of John Wilkins," Jorge Luis Borges
describes a Chinese Encyclopedia, in which it is written that all plants
and animals may be divided into:

I. THOSE THAT BELONG TO THE EMPEROR

A cat sweeping dawn into the corners
of the City. Pheasants with black heads
and necks squared in crimson that warble
and cluck when tossed grain. Sable antelope
clacking their horns among willow branches
by the river. Trumpet vine, heliotrope, the red
bird of paradise. Flies spinning above sliced
melon. Ten thousand rhododendrons and
the green writhing of dahlias. Globe-eyed carp
among saucers of hyacinth. The dragon
of morning and evening. Gibbons and
the orangutan that haunts the trees beyond
the terrace. Hornbills and buntings.
The raffish pose of the frill-necked lizard.
Mackerel and tuna stacked on ice. Mandrills
like clowns. Three stags and a decomposing body
laid out on a slab. Binturong. Bromeliad.
Clownfish and anemones. Five thousand butterflies
and one lepidopterist. A family of yak.

Tiger lilies with their mouths full of bees.
The clouded leopard that hunts mice and frightens
the horses. Cattle. Roses and the spring litter
of cherry trees. Cattails, irises, the emerald heads
of pintail ducks. Anything the heart desires:
a bat in a cage without a door. Tiny elephants
and the lizards that hunt them. Glass frogs,
their visible hearts hammering through their skin.
Lungfish. Spiders the size of books. A handful
of stones and two eggs of unknown origin.

II. THOSE DRAWN WITH A VERY FINE CAMEL'S HAIR BRUSH

It's not what I thought, not matted mohair
shaved from the gamy flank and Mr. Camel,
the inventor, not named for the harelip,
for the split toes, for the godawful smell
and the knees swollen as breadfruit.
Not *ata Allah*—God's gift—with its boat-
rolling gait. Not the ropey tail.
Rather, it's the ox or the goat,
squirrel or pony, *carcasses* abandoned
for the delicacy of a *caress*. Remains
as in affirmation, as in a man stroking
the cheekbones of his telescope's mirror
on the high balcony, the city painted up
around him like the caves at Lascaux,
tinted bulls in ocher and carmine,
the bird-headed man scorched in cinnamon
and the swimming stags. True stars
extinct in the city, the night sky gone
the color of sun-baked asphalt, a welter
of traffic rivering beneath his feet,
he watches a man and a woman undress
each other down the barrel of 3rd Avenue,
their several shadows burned onto the wall
as with the delicacy of a camel's hair brush.

III. THOSE THAT ARE TRAINED

The dog behind the fence is a symbol
for desire, for the anywhere-but-here grit
on the teeth found up the endless swerve
of river road high at the end of the valley.
The bent paneling, creased as tar
in the den, where the blue suede
from the small black-and-white
fills the room and the only channel
on this late is a gospel station
where a preacher mutters and sweats
then gut punches a man whose cancer
has returned, the paneling says something
too about desire as the room
goes gravel-colored with smoke,
the remains of a dimebag on a black
album striped by the full spectrum.
But leave them now, these two boys
who might be you and me, these boys
made up of memory and ash
and smoke, these two boys who have
the TV turned down and *Dark Side*
cranked again and the alarms are
detonating and the bells and the clock
tick-tocks like a damaged heart and
it all seems at once easy and impossible

because the road down valley is the only road
to everywhere as the dog barks and barks
and will never, ever, shut the fuck up.

IV. FABULOUS ONES

This poem is brought to you by the letter C.

Cattle egret, Big Bird says, *cetacean*,
the word squeaking like wet whale skin.

Big Bird keeps it real—his thug-life strut.

Do you like giants?
Only the small ones, the boy says.

Chinese catfish, cassava, cassowary.

He's an intellectual, spends his days off
in coffeehouses, crossing and uncrossing
the long orange tubes of his legs, discussing

Chomsky, conditional freedom, and *Cervantes*

with anyone who will listen. He marches
against the war, a thousand people
at his back, chanting

Catastrophe, cruise missile, children.

Big Bird refuses to fly south for the winter,
puts on his scarf, and heads out the door.

You can't fool me, the boy says.
I know Big Bird's not real.
It's just a suit with a little bird inside.

V. MERMAIDS

She comes ashore alone, humping
through the surf like an elephant seal.

Waves slam on the flat sand and the hillside's
afire with Christmas lights swagged

on piled balconies, the beach half-canyoned
by the high-rises ripping up the sky.

Her whiskers drip like piss, six flabby tits
down her chest, but her voice, when

she opens up that clam-can mouth,
comes on like Nina Simone's, gargantuan,

as the sand flies tear at her wrists
bent backwards on the sand. No one

comes out from the condos on the shore—
Tommy Dorsey's on the radio and the news

comes on at five. A corona of gulls tears
at plastic sacks dreadlocked in her hair

as she funnels into the chorus
what might be of *Love Me or Leave Me*

alone on a swollen tongue of beach.
The surprising velocity of dusk as the light fails.

VI. STRAY DOGS

gather behind the zoo
  to test the fence
and run the antelope,
  skittish the gazelles,
and scatter the dawning
  flamingos. In the morning
small bleating sheep
  shy from the carcass
of their own, entrails
  running bloody ribbons
along the corn and sawdust
  floor. A pronghorn's
haunch glazed with flies
  half-buried in the leaves,
but the dogs are long gone,
  hiding, bramble-tied,
curled in sleep, the day
  rotten with light
as the sun piles up the sky.

VII. THOSE THAT TREMBLE AS IF THEY WERE MAD

Sunlight slits into the mist which lingers
      in the forest, leaves
            so jittery with the pulse
    of dripping water their shadows
            tremble on the forest floor

and a hummingbird—a green violet-ear—haunts
      the lilac-blazed path
            down the Rio Savegre valley
    where in stock ponds trout rib the water
            with interlocking loops as they rise

towards a late hatch of stonefly.
      The bird's incomprehensible heart
            hammers up into the rafters
    of its chest as its black tongue wires
            the blossoms from below,

and what this has to do with knowledge,
      who can say? Madness could be
            the road down canyon,
    laddered switchbacks testing the gearbox,
            could be coffee plantations

woven into the cliffside, the crimson *pointillisme*
of the fruit against
the waxy leaves. But benevolence
must be the oceanic color of the tear
that streaks the emerald iridescence,

must be the act of naming
this bird for the sea—*Colibri thalassinus.*
Far from the shore,
the clouds' surf breaks against the coast
of the cordillera far below.

VIII. THOSE THAT ARE *NOT* INCLUDED IN THIS CLASSIFICATION

Just as Don Quixote,
crumpled as laundry
and laid out across

the Spanish *paisaje*,
pukes up into the face
of Sancho Panza,

and Sancho, hovering
and concerned for his
oafish, wounded lord,

follows suit and pukes down
into the face of the man
who promised him

a garden ripe with cockatoos
and the fleshy erotics
of the seabreeze,

so the black tulips
stunned with carmine or
a gaudy wisp of violet rip

through the leaf-litter, swing
and knock against each other
like mallets. It's spring

and the new sun, the lawn
paved with fat platters
of magnolia blossoms.

The wind rises and shreds
Sancho's island of sunlight
and fog, the galloping

surf of the rough, windward coast
where the name of every lost creature
gets written on pages of air,

where the dodo chuckles and grunts,
where the ivory-billed woodpecker
jackhammers long-leaf pine,

and dusky seaside sparrows
metronome marsh grass down
the scoured, dune-heavy shore.

IX. EMBALMED ONES

Take the body into the tent,
wash it with palm wine
and rinse in the water of the Nile.

> *Rats and cats sacked*
> *in freeze-dried packs.*

Cut into the left side, always left,
and gather all organs save
the heart—it will be needed.

> *Sliced sections of a human head*
> *suspended in green fluid.*

With bronze hooks inserted
up the sinuses and through
the ethmoid bone, a twist of

> *A Gobi bear, a camel fetus, that two-headed*
> *dog with its permanent snarl,*

the wrist is all it takes to extract
the brains. Rub the body with natron.
Stuff with sawdust, leaves and linen—

and all the species
in the genus Arctocephalus.

it can be made quite lifelike.
After forty days, wash again with wine
and myrrh. Wrap in linen, alternating

Baboons, birds, and crocodiles.
Sacred bulls in their own cemetery at Sakkara.

coats of resin. A priest will perform
the rites to Open the Mouth. Now
the body can eat and drink, smell

Hunger preserved in a collection
of sheep stomachs,

the flowers of the afterlife, taste the names
of the fruits of the dead. The heart remains
inside waiting for its counter weight—

the last Tasmanian wolf
dead in a Hobart zoo.

X. SUCKLING PIGS

This encyclopedia of articulate nothing,
taxonomy of damage, library of sand.
Manuscript of clouds, archipelago of crabs
in a wash of seafoam. I could write anything—
a pack of pigs sucking at the blank canvas
of the sow's belly—and you'd believe it.

XI. OTHERS

The rainbow hits the water hard,
     a spray of color almost physical—
wind rich and horizontal
     from the west—rain tearing
  gnarled waves, coconut froth
and ratty, wet raffia in the soup.

The ocean's the conclusion
     to the clumsy whisper of names
we read onto the land—hummock, tussock,
     beach, spit, strand. No words
  for the choppy shove of the waves,
the ache they leave on the sand slipping away.

Lianas, waree palm, mahogany.
     The estuary humming with the tongues
of many rivers—*Chirripo, Sierpe, Suerte*—
     as rana con blue jeans,
  the blue jeans frog (*Dendrobates pumilio*),
thumbnail small in the tannin muck

and fishtail palm, trills its delicate Morse.
     All that language tunneling into
  the steaming earth as the sun returns,
     awkward somehow, this business.

We live in the words we use,
says Wittgenstein, so what to make

of the parataxis of genus and species—
        the Latin running underneath it all,
    electric life of a dead language
        translated here to the tri-color of exile?
    A large brunette bird whistles
and pops as it hunts in the crown of palms.

In English it's Montezuma's Oropendula
        and the Latin's pure gold: *Psarocolius montezuma.*
    At night green sea turtles return
        to nest on this eponymous coast,
    heads down in the wracked sand, laboring
with their winged, inarticulate hands.

Chelonia mydas, their owlish eyes tear up
        in the desiccate air. Sea oats
    toss their blond hair. They see little
        beyond sand tented with driftwood
    but gasp with beaked mouths as if drowning
in the incomprehensible surf of the wind.

XII. INNUMERABLE ONES

How to count? Begin with one, or $n + 1$
where n is the number of ants in a colony,
and 1 is you looking over your own shoulder,
looking into the earth, driving a stick down
into the mound like a gifted chimp, pulling it out
to count the inscrutable bodies, huge-headed
warriors sawing the wood. Where n is bacteria
and 1 is your colon, the wealth of *E. coli*
colonizing and shifting upriver, where n
is the burger you ate yesterday and 1 is you
heaving into the sink and falling back
wracked with fever. Where n is brine shrimp
and 1 the stink they make on a hot day,
the light above the Great Salt Lake gone flat
and gauzy. Where n is the caribou cresting
across the Porcupine in the Yukon and n^2
the mosquitoes that blind them—eyes jammy
with crushed bodies—and drive them mad.
Where 1 is the Cessna and the rifle,
where 1 is the bullet and the carcass
resting on the tundra's mossy sponge.

XIII. THOSE THAT HAVE JUST BROKEN A FLOWER VASE

Because some birds land only to nest,
because they travel through the canyon's
half-light like science fiction standards,
the swerve and veer through a dangerous chute,
because down valley the landscape fades
to a geometric test of wills—algebraic
agriculture arguing with the river's
floodplain calculus—because the clouds
branch and froth in blossom above
the Allegheny Mountains, because
these peaks have been lifted up
and torn down three times, because
exhaustion writes its name in deer trails
across the smoky hillsides in midwinter,
because beauty walks hand in hand
with grief, because it's the only time
she'll ever see one, I'll talk about
the collared swift that died in flight
(family name *Apodidae*—without feet)
and landed in my neighbor's pachysandra.
The picture window rang where
it smacked the glass. Framed in the casement,
her husband drops to his knees in the March-wet
earth, a stroke blooming up the branches
in his head. At least that is how I choose

to imagine it—the gelling of the narrative
around the low tone of rung glass,
the warm carcass of the bird splayed
in the elegant green of the new shoots,
his dead-arm slump as the cat, startled, drops
from the pie chest and knocks a bud vase
from its place. So, as she turns to find
the door, she sees them both there
suspended in midair, with the grace
of everything about to shatter.

XIV. THOSE THAT LOOK LIKE FLIES FROM A DISTANCE

Start simply—
        the dead snag filled
with white herons near Caño Blanco,
the muscular press of clouds above,
the colonnade a plane slices into
and the sudden smallness of the plane
seen from the ground, farmers
looking up from their fields of aloe,
the plants like rows of jade octopi
and the pearl buttons on their shirts
iridescent as flies. A bottle hive
of paper wasps hanging from
the middle story treetops along
the road to San Isidro becomes
the eye of a gazelle gone gauzy and fly-
charmed on the hot savannah below
a hillside glossy with wildebeest.
Pink dolphins roiling blackwater
as they herd tucunare within the flooded
forest turn to squadrons of toucans
streaming through back-lit kapoks,
long-tendriled lianas, the silver-edged
leaves of the winter's bark trees
school in the wet air like herring.
Plankton bloom in the cold upwelling

of the Chukchi Sea. Shrimp feed
so delicately on the plankton
and sand eels gorge on the shrimp.
I close the book where I have been writing
all day; the unused pages fall whitely
over the City. *What have you learned?*
The words churn, a mob of bitterns
thrash about the corpse of a marten,
hagfish writhe on a gray whale one mile
down as leaf-cutter ants dismember
a nearby *guanacaste* and moths punish
the porchlight. Shoals of starlings
awash in a mackerel sky, small as
the rain that comes on in the distance.

UNDERWHELMED

Under the catastrophic dark,
the comet splintering the sky
with its ancient grief,
under the splay-handed palms,
under drinks glowering dark in
globes of glass, under the tender
humidity, the phosphorescent surf,
under the calls of nightjars
chuckling up from the ground,
under the ticking aloe under the moon's
absence, *under, under, under.*
Under the blinking stripes jets
write across the sky, under
stillness, the cabin pressure holding
steady, under the coned light
blanking out pages of gloss, under
the plunge of my love's hair, under
her sadness and her eyes
startling as stars, under our lives,
the miscarried child left in the bowl,
underground, underwater, understory,
under the bougainvillea's whorish musk,
under the coral's forest of horn, under
God, undertow, underdog, under
everything there is a season,
under the absence of twilight,
under the beach's grittle and bone,

under the words, *startle, startle,*
under the luxury of the table
so whitely laid, under
the candle's light shaped
like a hanging blade, we tear
apart the body of the fish and leave
glistening ladders of bone.

QUO VADIS?

. . . when you are old you will stretch out your hands, and another
will gird you and take you where you do not want to go.

—JOHN 21:18-19

The woman with the invisible stigmata
sits day by day in the *gelateria* and wonders
why no one else can see what she cannot,

though she knows her hands are carved
with holes, knows they are a blessing,
a punctured prompt that says suffering

is more than cars sizzling past in the drizzle,
history more than layered sediment in stone,
the tomb of a talking crow and Simon Peter

running from his execution. *Quo vadis?* he asks
the risen Lord who passes. When the answer
is a return to Rome and a second crucifixion,

Peter turns back to find his own death upside down.
Such stories are not to be trusted, she thinks.
Who asks for such a thing? A string of pain to tie

your eyes to. Eye your ties to, says the crow.
The rain keeps coming and the city has gone quiet.
The woman with the invisible stigmata hears

the crow call her name. She palms napkins stained
with flames of *mora e cioccolato* as men in black
waiting out the storm beneath the awning

pass their flat wit back and forth like cigarettes.
Children heave themselves into the rain.
A bouquet of umbrellas blossoms from their hands.

for Tony & Penelope

LANDSCAPE WITH PIGEONS AND
THE TREE OF HEAVEN

When the sun skates behind the spire of the cathedral,
When that shadow paints a finger across the square where
      the flower vendor with daffodils in buckets sits
      in the new dark beneath the awning of the bank,
When the cars pause and the human traffic spills and gathers
      as oil above flame's blue petals buoying the black edges
      of a sauté pan,
When a woman passes flashing the sudden springtime
      of her thighs beneath kick pleats and piping,
When the world seems elegant and wet with promise,
      a corona of fire painted around the spire
      and tombstone arches of light from the bell tower
      paved into the square,
And, equally, when the sentimental gloss of sunlight is called
      into question by its absence,
When newspapers menace the fence as construction rumbles
      tectonically beyond the black-plastic sheeting,
And the grimy mitts of feral pigeons (*Columba livia*) chortle
      and bob their puffed, oiled iridescence beneath
      the ailanthus, chased by children with handfuls of corn,
I am reminded that in Chinese the ailanthus is the Tree
      of Heaven and pigeons are called the *clumsy bird*,
      relative of the dodo and other flightless doves
      extinct on islands across the Pacific,
I am reminded that the birds are symbol, the spirit in flames
      descending on the head of Christ, counterpart

to the water of desire John drizzled upon his head,
I am reminded, too, that lovers should refrain from their consumption
    (said Martial, *Who would be lusty should not eat this bird*)
And that when Christ finally drove the traders from the temple,
    pigeons rose off the tables and swept the sky clean
    with their wings.

BLIND DESIRE

The *O* as in an open door, the *I will be there.*
Vanity, vanity. The circling around,
as in absence (in Latin, it's *from the stars*).

A feathered harp of winter sumac strummed
by water along the flooded river. A walkway
damp with fog, stairs that climb until they vanish.

Roads bustle with absent traffic, the mutter of all
conversations that have yet to happen, two
bodies cinched together at the gluttonous mouth.

§

Two bodies woven into a twisted
biography of trees. Creepers and trunks,
the sudden canary fire of forsythia

blazing up hillsides. The birdhouse stuffed
with wire, mud, and grass. The whinny
of the robins above the whiskey-

scented mulch. The landscape collapses
into limbs. Spring leaves lie down,
small hands stroking the grass.

§

Summer's leafy design dismantled
by a week's chill rain to a damp thatch
beneath the trees. She has vanished

up the stairs to sleep as the house creaks
in the cold stink of the wind—waiting
for the snow to come, waiting for its gargantuan

quiet to fall upon my life. The tv buzzing
technicolor: beer bottles, dead soldiers,
the found poem of the silver moon.

§

A winter moon hung in the daylight sky.
The back cove. Three miles in twenty minutes,
breath like the body itself frothing out before me.

The tide pulls out and a bright wind blows in-
land, a scum of ice cauliflowered in the water.
Black backs and eider ducks rock in rafts

upon the water. The sun wets the limestone
on the path it touches and my love lies and lies
in a corridor of firelight stroking her hair.

§

Her hair, the cleft of his mouth,
the arc of her breast, stiff tension
in the loins—two bodies

working together in the moon-
striped dark. The traffic that passes
paints a strange geometry

across the ceiling, their eyes closed
to the light of such terrible pleasure.
Pleasure. Then the falling away.

§

Fog on the river falling away, the spillway
smoothed over. Blue tarps tent the bank.
Empty dock pilings spike the water where

the flood ripped boats from their cleats
and the planks from their pilings.
The river sediments a stratum of loss

along the bank, plastic like raffia plaited
through the trees. All the world in flux:
the heart a hatbox full of eels.

§

Fairy houses of stick and bark, hatbox
and four-square, toy-subdivision
frosted nacreous with mussel shells.

Death-head juniper berries, tiny geography
of hope blocked out across a pine-streaked
half acre. Alone on the scraped granite

shore—she's gone. The wind-sculpted
spruce and black oak semaphore offshore.
The cold ocean, the sculpted world.

§

A sculpture of gulls on the tarmac, heads
pinned against the wind, the cold light
gray as the cloudcover that drapes

the russet hills. Spring begins
in the smallest argument of green. Desire
follows and what it feeds on, flush as the water

over the spillway, the foursquare skeleton
of the steelworks rust-blasted below
the overpass and the sky, battered open.

§

The sky as red as rose-tinged flesh,
like sex-flushed skin, the chestnut broken
beneath my boot. The lilac thrums

with hummingbirds blazing into flight,
a hillside orchard of inedible apples.
Dawn-blushed peaches rot on the ground.

Dusk lights up the hills along the river,
clouds lit like snowcover above. Laughter
from the open mouths of other people's houses.

§

The mouths of the blooming
trees, a warm wind comes down,
the brown earth rapt with petals,

thin skin of henna. Rain avenues
down from the asphalt sky, glitters
like galaxies in the grass.

Beware, Josephine, wrote Napoleon,
beware. One fine night the door
will be broken down and I will be there.

ARS POETICA WITH PAIN

In this one, Yosemite Sam gets hung. Bugs digs
his way into the prison yard after he missed

that mythical left at Albuquerque and soon Sam's big hat flaps
in the wind, his knee-high, shitkickers jerking in midair.

It's not Eurydice stumbling into ecstasy up the moss-
tumbled steps, Orpheus erect before her;

it's not Bugs smacking carrots as the fade circles down
around him and the cursive loops across the screen—

craft and the hero victorious in the common tongue.
All the strange grammars of success yield

the elastic cat who balloons back to wholeness
after being smacked with the frying pan,

or the duck that slips his bill back across his jaw
after eating a load of buckshot. Never the scene

when Elmer Fudd blotches his crotch with piss
when Bugs readies to take his kneecaps

with his own shotgun. In this one, Eurydice
chews on a worm of pain that sounds like *farewell*

to Orpheus, untuned to the choral music of Hell
and Orpheus' head, cast aside, floats forever singing.

In this one, the Thracian women toss the broken lyre,
mangled as a smashed racket, into the fire and smile

as smoke ropes up around their throats
and the strings hiss and curl into ampersands.

STALIN ON STAGE

The angelic gilt of the ceiling lit
with stage-light imitation, fractured
surf of the goldleaf pouring across
the proscenium, the aging rafters,
the crowd speckled with reflection:
all this brings us to Stalin.
Stalin on stage. To the moment
when he has just finished speaking
and the audience rises in unison
to collapse the air with their applause.
Minutes pass and no one will stop,
the very air threatened by the noise,
until one general, veteran of wars
and Tannenberg, an armada
of ribbons blockading the deep Baltic
of his uniform, drops his hands and sits.
We know the history so we know
the story now, before it's given.
How he is rousted and pummeled
at dawn and the trees in a cold grove
gather round him as the rifles rise.
Never be the first to stop applauding Stalin,
he is told, before the guns' ovation
rises up into the glacial sky, birdcall
returning after a brief silence. This
is wrong, as I return to the source
to reread the history, the general just

an owner, his paper factory offering up
the forms that will be filled out to detail
the reams of his misfortune. He wasn't
killed, wasn't turned out into the morning
trees and introduced to the tiny mouths
of twenty weapons. He was given ten
years in the gulag, ten years at labor
in the flesh-splitting cold, ten years
in the joy of short sunlight. *Ten years*.
Does that make it better or worse?

On his release, his daughter's there
to collect him, and they hobble into
the flat March light, holding on to
each other in the Riga station.
The train pulls at them as it leaves,
the sound of its wheels on the ties
at the crossing like men beating a horse
with boards. The train that once
carried the poem's moral center
vanishes into a cold drizzle that falls
on their necks, gilds their hair with dew
the hue of piss, almost the color
of the wash of gold above Stalin,
who remains, of course, up on stage
beneath the clarion lights and seraphs,
his face bright as paper, drenched
in the warmth of the applause
that somehow never dies.

BEFORE TRINITY

a conflagration that would overturn
the palace of the sky
—OVID

In white sands anchored by sage
and ocotillo, a cactus wren,

its small black eye a small black world
burning, alights and doesn't know its life

counts only minutes now before it turns
to a puff of jellied fire. The woman

navigating the canyons beyond *Ojo Caliente*,
headlights draped across the pendular hills,

kids slapped across the backseat,
senses none of this as static overtakes her radio

and her horn-rims reflect a tiny brightness
past the horizon. She's been driving all night,

the silver silo of coffee thrust between her thighs.
She doesn't know safety's a matter of the odds

now that the world's been made that much more
savage. In hours, her children will wake

and stretch with stupid, sleep-filled mouths
and gape at the dry washes and sagey hillsides,

the land stunned with sunlight. The boys
will stagger off to piss in the clean dawn,

thin streams of gold wire tying them
to the earth, and they will barely feel

the small finery of ash that lands on
their eyelashes and dusts their faces like wings.

AMAZON PARABLE

The bees that will strip every hair
from your head instead of swelling
your hands with a thatch of venom,

that will leave you bald and clean
and unstung, they are my subject
today. Whether this hive, cylindrical

and birchy, lie or not, the shape of threat
that hangs above the white river
south of Iquitos in the meandering fan

of the Tahuayo, whether this hive houses
such hazard can't matter. The story carries
its own weight, as does the ass that carried

Christ off the Mount of Olives,
its sweat-worked back, the rope-burn
that pinks its muzzle. It stands

beneath the awful sun as the pigeons
explode from the temple in a flaring
of white wings and slapping. But this

was never about the ass, really, or the fig tree
withered beneath the hand but the weight
the story carries—told in the boat as we

thrum upriver—the strange menace of power,
the shearing leaving you stripped
to flushed flesh beneath gaudy palms
ticking above, fanning you, blessing you.

THE BELFAST NOTEBOOKS: POEMS AND PROSE

(2017)

LED ZEPPELIN DEBUTS
"STAIRWAY TO HEAVEN,"
ULSTER HALL, MARCH 5, 1971

. . . more than 900 were killed that night
and half the homes in Belfast destroyed.

—BBC

The crowd waits, ready to burst into anything but this
slow-motion wreck of an intro they've never heard before

with its swaying guitar and that recorder floating
out of the dark like Irish pipes, and now some jostle

to the bar in the back, talking over the top of
this strange *lady who's sure all that glitters is gold*

and into the white faces on the tops of their pints,
while one girl—spattered with paisley and red beads

like stopped droplets of blood—sways back and forth
before the stage (the tempo and the reefer in perfect

harmony now) and no longer wonders about
this man with blunt hands and manners short

as his hair, this man she recently started thinking of
as her love, no longer wonders when he will return

to put his arms around her in the clumsy way
she finds endearing but suspects that—if it lasts—

she will come to loathe, and then the lights drop
and Plant sweeps the golden blitz of his hair

across his eyes in echo of the gold leaf sparkling
across the ceiling like the small and distant fires

of homes burning in the hills all around him
as if it is Easter Tuesday, 1941, again, and

the American soldiers whose children will gather
like druids around any turntable playing this song

suddenly find themselves in darkness and silence
as air-raid sirens squeal up into the distant hills,

the city unprepared for it (no searchlights accusing
the cloud-speckled sky, no chuff of anti-aircraft)

and because there is nothing to be done and nowhere
to go, Delia Murphy, up on stage in chiffon and lace

as bombs begin their soft percussion
in the distance, says, "We're not going anywhere,"

and drops into "Bye Bye Blackbird" as one soldier
gathers the small bouquet of an Irish girl in his arms

and swings her onto the bare runway of the dance floor—
this floor that will collapse twice in years to come

beneath dancers pounding their lives into it with all
the rhythm the small hammers of their feet can manage,

but not this night, no, not tonight—and now other
soldiers drop their need, their dread urgency

to do *something* and follow his lead, gathering
their own girls from the garden of faces along the wall

and soon the floor is swirling and Murphy is singing,
Make my bed and light the light, I'll be home late tonight,

bombs dropping across the city from a flotilla of diesel
and gear, dropping down alleyways carved into the air,

and they dance on into the night, hour after hour
as clouds and blaze swirl up throughout the city

like flirtatious color gels spinning paisley and psychodelia
across the scene, Plant picking up the tempo now,

buckets of drumbeats dropped at his feet, Page's guitar
rising on the upbeats, and the lights pound

and the sound rises and the crowd finally engages,
boys returning from the bar in waves like aircraft

coasting above a defenseless, darkened city and
when he does return and slide his arms around her,

his hands meaty as peat, she will smile and think him
wonderful, aware only of his hands and the music

and the ripe crush of the crescendo as it breaks
across them both, together there on that fragile floor,

not knowing, of course, that he will die in McGurk's
in December of that very year, die beneath a wall

brought down by another bomb, brought down
out of some terrible and ongoing heaven.

NEW FACES OF BELFAST

It's 1972, the year the Ambassador finally
closes, the theater's cathedral arches rigid
in the fall's afternoon gloom, asphalt a small
galaxy of shattered glass and graffiti duct-
working walls, and *What's New Pussycat?*
still sparkles on the marquee—as if
the world's a many-roomed mansion split
between paisley and pinstripe, a bacchanal
and carnival that will not last the night—

but there is this question of the new faces
that appeared overnight smeared on plywood
sheeting locking in the construction site
next door, these new faces of Belfast,
wanted posters like promos for a film yet
to come starring Murphy and the leaders
of the Shankill Butchers horse-brushed
to the wall with a glue of broken glass
to separate the blood from a man's hands
should he try and pull them from the wall;

these faces tell a story that will take years
to finish, a story called abduction and extremity,
a story called hard man and kneecapper,
a story called trouble. Many will die wearing
shirts of their own blood when they've heard it,
but today we know what we know and

it is little. Today the marquee's lights trickle
on merrily and the eyes of the posters mark
dark knots in the wood. Today jackdaws
lift their gray hoods above the roofline
and night lies down along the Falls Road.

CERTAIN THINGS HERE ARE QUIETLY AMERICAN

—DEREK WALCOTT

The fence and wall, the town divided
the way a clock is divided by time
as the Lough cuts the one o'clock hour
from its face. All the missing trains.
Parking lots chock-a-block by eight
surrounding savage, seventies architecture
where foxglove breaks pavement with
a will unlike the old Irish backstory.
The Apple Store shining like the church
of all things modern. Mute factories
brittle with webs of broken windows
where workers once walked down
from East Belfast with overalls and pails
then stepped up late afternoon to the rail
for a few jars before slumping uphill
home in the long graying of dusk to wives
whose day was made of muscling water
into flax at the river's edge. Dockyards
abandoned with the want of urban space,
piers slapped by the seawater wake
tossed by the hulking ferry that glows white
as it churns up the lough. Dog-faced seals
that raise their untroubled heads to watch

the ship pass through the gunmetal gap
the sea plows through these Antrim hills,
fields divided stone by stone on either shore.

VAN MORRISON PERFORMS "SOMETIMES WE CRY" WITH HIS DAUGHTER, ODYSSEY ARENA, BELFAST

Morrison, eh? our cab driver asks, not really asking, as we're driving through Shaftsbury Square and the collapse of old churches down to this new Odyssey which hovers like a lit ship beside the shore.

He forgets where he comes from, so he does, the driver continues, as we pass an old wall camouflaged by a mural of red hands that flank a masked gunman. This wall painted with scarlet fists like all the small roses of rage. This wall that warns—YOU ARE NOW ENTERING LOYALIST SANDY ROW—as the Union Jacks accumulate along the street beneath the rain.

In the gauzy wasteland of myth, one man wanted this island so desperately that he separated his hand from his arm with his own sword and heaved the flaccid crab of it from his ship to the rocky shore to win the race to first put skin on Ulster, so now red hands mark a bloody map spattered on buildings across the city.

Inside the Odyssey, by the time his daughter slides out from behind the risers to sing "Sometime We Cry," a song that now sounds to me like the true duet of the North, Van's easy Irish soul has come and gone like a home left long ago. They stand together, both of them downstage like two worlds joined: her voice gossamer as a thin cloud in the long blue collapse of day over the Lough added to the brackish, black estuary of his jazz growl.

The piano builds a pier out across the water for them to cross and they wander out to where the sunrise of their voices builds an island in the air and the surf bothers the bird-churned shore and the unending oak forest, a perpetual home glossed with the lace of breaking waves.

Back here in Belfast, the lough is colored with the sky's gray flannel and small gardens struggle beside the row houses—new paint covering whitewash mottled like a map of an old, old world. Stones assemble along the shore, stones that writhe with hundreds of crabs like a collection of severed hands, and all the stars are hidden.

They finish the song and wave to us in front of the dark altar of the drums as the rough surf of applause beats down on them. The past has become its own Ithaca and that island on the horizon hovers still. Their two hands join at the edge of the stage, lit up as if they are wearing history's bloody glove and the future's long white dress.

STROKE CITY

Here the police patrol in squads of seven—full military formation, one man on point and one woman sweeping, turning again to check her six—as I search for my family's Presbyterian Church. Locked-down walls built long ago frame the old town and the oak grove at the top that the city is named for. St. Columb's cathedral stands overwhelmed with Union Jacks for July as the Orange Order gatehouse supervises Bogside tenements where murals recall Bloody Sunday and Operation Motorman.

For a town nicknamed Stroke City—the slash between the English and the Irish, capitol and plantation, the eternal face-off and a city divided, town signs painted over again and again to read ~~LONDON~~/derry in a palimpsest of rage and repetition—all this makes sense.

Did I tell you that we came through here? My people, I mean. William, his name was, and he was planted like some kind of root stock the English hoped would spread, tenacious as ribbon grass, with the other Scots to control the last of the Irish chieftains. But what he found was Anne, a catholic wife from Donegal, and a city where neither were welcome.

When I find his Church, it's a minor thing. Might as well be a bank now. Doric columns and the high windows framing the façade beneath the glazed light of the late sun.

He would have seen the beginnings of it all—civil wars and a time called trouble—here on the Grand Parade where 14 sycamores (one each for the apprentice boys who locked a gate on the imminent Jacobite king) now line walls he walked between the Hangman's bastion and the Coward's where, when the siege went bad and even rats were scarce and the hides of horses tasted of slaughter, it was easiest to escape. But I see only a little.

William escaped, that's true and all I know, as the soldiers turn the corner ahead of me, cautious as cats, and sycamores drop thousands of tiny keys across the walls of the city. I have returned in hope of finding a way in through the locked door of this story—how he must have walked with Anne, her hand resting on his arm, watching the sun break open clouds coming up out of the west and talking softly about a new world.

for my father, and his before him

SELF-PORTRAIT IN NINE GENERATIONS

William strides out of the Glasgow dusk,
long-legged in the summer light that only fails
late into the night, and then he gathers Anne,
his new wife, from Donegal, as if she were
a basket of fruit, a gift to bring to his new hosts,
and then he's here in Philadelphia (on paper
it seems so easy—we can ignore the three-month
thrashing in steerage, puking in the dripping dark)
and James will follow, a son, an American, he thinks,
after all there's revolution on every broadside
slapped against the board and batten, horse-
brushed with glue, and he's a glass maker
whose specialty is floats for fishing nets—
the Gulf of Maine and the banks still roiling with cod
—and then just as suddenly there will be
Alexander who barely remembers William,
just a face edged with white, the smell of a pipe;
in fact, Alexander rarely thinks that far back
(he's still young and he's crossed the mountains
and there's a continent spread out before him
like the cloth spread across the table before
the plates of ox-tail and eels and the glazed-brown
goose are all laid down) and he has 9 children,
one of whom will be my great-great-great-grandfather,
and the print-shop he runs and Pennsylvania summers
go by so fast, and his children, who couldn't remember

if asked, spread out down river and over and that's
the past and this is a new world, and he's tired now—
the day's nearly done and the world's shrinking back
on him as his cataracts turn the world to milk and gauze—
and the almost-Scottish hills shoulder up into a sky
that carries the light of day long after the sun has set.

WATERCOLOR PAINTING CLASS

Once a week above the rooftops
of Queen's Quarter—skylights
and chimneypots providing
the order the eye asks for—inside
an old girls school turned studio
where I was the youngest student
in a class retired long ago from
daily life in Belfast, checkpoints
and rifles, parades and old enemies
in mask and balaclava, pressure
of a city mounting toward the fires
of July, I worked my morning into
gardens of amaryllis and lily,
small pastoral welcome of geese
among outbuildings gray and streaked
as the rain crashed its shrapnel
on the exhaust vents for the kilns,
and, one day, as the sky crawled by
in its uniform of grim and somber,
I painted a close-up of the small star
of a sunflower with the all the colors
of the light I'd missed that winter,
filling the canvas with warm petals
of citron and blonde, champagne
and canary, and, at the heart of it all,
the black of the seedpod ready to explode.

THE MONA LISA OF BELFAST

The Mona Lisa is as famous for her weird ability to follow you
with her eyes as she is for her puzzling smile.
—JOSH CLARK

In this mural, no vast landscape
swaddles into the distance,
no rivers braid a chalked savannah
of hills, no glossy lake, no road
toward a glimmer of pastoral ease.
In this mural, a gunman with one eye
closed and the gun pointed right
at you, this enigma in a black hood,
this air of menace in the face
turned to face you, the flat motley
of camo, crossed Union Jacks,
and the raised rifle sight
that follows you through
the *sfumato* of Shankill field
(this orchard of ruin with
a no-man's land inside it).
Here there is just this message—
Quis Separabit?—clear as smashed
glass across this pitch and plain
as the red hand of Ulster,
bloody mitt not yet a fist,
this message and the gun sight

that follows you everywhere,
its simple, single eye tracking you
even as you try to leave through
rare sunlight speckling the open gate.

SAMSON AND GOLIATH

And all I ever learned of love
Was to shoot at someone who outdrew you.
—LEONARD COHEN

On the Lagan, close by the weir in Belfast—
my wounded city sewn together with
the chain-link stitching of fences—
the twin, canary brackets of Harland
and Wolff's huge shipyard gantry cranes
(named for giants overcome at the height
of their strength) line up like sutures and
the eye's needle draws out and through
to the patched-up hillsides beyond
as if sewing together the murky layerings

of history. You've heard the stories
I'm sure—Goliath who stood before
the Israelites like living thunder.
Goliath who looted the Ark, carried it
to the temple at Dagon. Whose head
was carted off to Jerusalem by David
as if to say: *You're next, motherfuckers!*
Samson who tied torches to the tails
of foxes and let them free in the fields of
the Philistines. Samson who was deceived
by Delilah, who was shorn and blinded,
and forced to grind grain. Samson who

brought the temple at Dagon down
upon himself, thus ending the lesson—

and you could be forgiven for thinking
that lesson lost until 1970 when curfew
came down hard on the Falls Road
and four were shot dead and stones
fell from a sky of building fume and
CS gas melted tears out of the eyes
of anyone watching as petrol bombs
marked the line of British soldiers
into a frieze of black and rage.

The two flanks massed and simmered.
Nothing was resolved and nothing
was made clear until 3,000 women
with their children marched up
the Falls and crossed that barricade
carrying nothing but bags of groceries.

Groceries. So maybe the stories
are wrong. Maybe Goliath walked
that sun-withered wash toward
David in hope of watching
his children age in peace. Maybe
Goliath was the ox-soft heart led
to slaughter for a new God who
shone alone like vengeance
in the heavens. Maybe Delilah
was the wine Samson was forbidden,
fruit of her, scent of ripe and union,
scent of clay and decay and sex
and peat that rises up from hillsides

here seamed by wall and rill.
Scent of two people coming
together to make a third as the rain
falls, smoothing the land to a shabby
fabric of stone and whin and cloud,
softening of the sky against which
those cranes stand, empty, like stitches
holding the patchwork greenery together.

for Zev Trachtenberg

SILENCE

When Ruan Pienaar lines up the kick, his eyes down
towards the small parcel he is trying to deliver
over the posts and into the heart of the south,
his thin, handsome face its own arena of concentration,
the pub goes hushed, a few hard *shush*es silencing
the chatter of those not paying enough attention
and now we are quiet as churchmen waiting to sing
our own hymn to the ball and the foot and the muscled
shoulder—"Stand Up for the Ulstermen"—waiting
to sing with our pints raised high, waiting in a deep
silence despite the fact the match happens away
across the Irish Sea, across history with its small
daily galas; we go silent as a field of grass before
a thicket of storm drops down over the Antrim Hills,
wind in the whin suddenly gone and off another way,
silent as the streets past the gasworks at two am,
silent as the Lagan canal and the linen mill, everyday
now as of a Sunday, broken windows like a brittle web
of damage that holds it all together, silent as Ravenhill;
we go as silent as we will, a few hours later,
after the match is over and Ulster has lost again,
when the young woman and her lover pick up
the pieces of a song that says love will conquer hate,
as if the two were teams opposed on a great pitch,
and play for each other, the man's hands stroking notes
out of the fiddle he rests beneath the shag of hair
he wears atop his glasses, the woman's voice settling

like a bird on each note before it rises into the pub's silence,
its arc like the arc of the rugby ball, lifting and lifting
into the long cobalt of dusk before it finally curves
away, missing the goal in a silence like the silence
that must have blossomed after the bomb went off
here in the Rose and Crown, a space that was suddenly
and forever six voices quieter, but that was years and years ago
and we have long since decided not to speak of such things.

STYLES OF HELL: A SEQUENCE
(SELECTIONS)

. . . you must descend. It is one of the styles.

—LARRY LEVIS

I. IN THE CONVENTO DI SAN FRANCESCO, FIESOLE, ITALY, ON THE 10ᵀᴴ ANNIVERSARY OF THE INVASION OF IRAQ

Above Firenze where the light in turns
takes on the color of lavender in urns
above the Piazza Mino and aged-gray,
Etruscan walls break through hillsides
of boxwood and bay as spires of cyprus
echoing the clocktower thrust through
gardens cultivated into a permanence
of orchid and wisteria, sprayed blessings
of pastel roses throttling the masonry,
at the bottom of a stepladder staircase
below the cloisters, you will find hell.

Not Dante's murderous burned alive
in a river of fire—*that stream of blood*
where those who injure others violently,
boil—but rather paintings that depict
a Chinese hell where demons-turned-
bureaucrat preside over peasants
exactly arranged for punishment, as if

horror were not in abuse but rather
in its orchestration. Not the scourging
demon stripping flesh from a man's back
with a whip of live cats, but a gentleman
pouring tea beneath a pagoda as women
wait in line to be churned into mince
by hell's waterwheel. Another forced
to count a perpetuity of passing insects
led to diners at eternal tables overflowing
in a hell without glowing weeps of flame
consuming flesh reborn each night.

The Franciscans arrived in Beijing
in 1590 to bring an Empire into the fold
of the lamb, but for a culture that feared
the methodical more, the traditional
torments of hell read like opium
dreams. Chinese style was the long
mind of the Emperor made of mandarins
and a tectonic shifting of paper smothering
their lives the way the resistance fighter
is devoured by the paperwork of the state.

So on the posters, up to bloated demons
behind their desks, come an eternity
of souls in the everdusk waiting to be
assigned severance. One hoards acres
of forms and another walks hell's thickets
with a clipboard and a lamp. A third
documents each cup of tea offered up
to women this close to becoming paste.
This is the style that becomes us now,
in the fresh garden of a new century,

where our task is to watch and
record those so precisely ransacked
in the luxuriant, civil-service of torture,
to watch and record, saying nothing.

Back above in my life, in the world where
gardens mark the boundaries of paradise,
smell of lavender and poppies blooming
like spattered tenderness—after all
this time—I have climbed into an orchard
of buddleias and ash, like Orpheus
back in his grove of oaks. I have tried
to find my way out, but what is once seen
cannot be otherwise and the trees
no longer have ears. Words of the dead
loiter in the air. This night's garden lies
heavy with their style beneath a paper sky,
the inked-in shadows, and distant light
dwindling into the bloody river of sunset.

II. JACOB'S LADDER, BATH, ENGLAND

Dodimedis has lost two gloves. He asks that the person who has stolen them should lose his mind and eyes in the temple.

   —curse written on a stone offered to the mother-goddess & recovered
   from the Bath thermal springs.

When Jacob lay down that night he placed a rock beneath his head—
fleeing Esau as he was, bereft and without succor below the racing

chariot of the sky—and slept and dreamt of ladders and angels
and years and days, dreamt of stairs and the sway between heaven

and earth and when Jacob awoke from his sleep he said, *Surely
the Lord is in this place; and I did not know it,* and named

that land Beth'el.
      But in Bath—
Roman town of golden stone and iron-hot water where curses

carved on rocks were cast into springs in the hope of the goddess's
revenge, namesake town for one in Maine where once on the rocky

accumulation of the shore I found a small stone with PROFOUND HURT
written across it in dark Sharpie—
         in Bath, the angels Jacob dreamed
clamber ladders on the façade of the Abbey toward statues

of Paul and Peter and sunset fires that limestone to flame,
the sun unbuckling the horizon's belt of cloud. Beth'el means

the house of God, and Bath was named for healing waters, but
the sky here is heavy as sediment (no nest of angels treed among

cirrus) and when someone casts a stone into the water asking for
the clarity of pain she feels to be brought down upon another

for a change, she is asking for the labor of angels to be delivered—

that dangerous interchange between heaven and earth
that rarely ends well for our all too human world—

asking for the goddess who lives in water and stone to give back
a piece of herself to one, bereft and without succor, alone

and dreaming on a rocky shore, who hopes for someone else
to be run down by the chariot of the lord for once,

and who will not know it, days or centuries later,
when the water returns that prayer, unanswered and forgiven.

III. YE OLDE TRIP TO JERUSALEM, NOTTINGHAM, ENGLAND

In the light that knifes through a thin window, I sit with a pint and a plate of cheese at a pub called the Trip whose name doesn't mean that exactly, but rather the opposite, because in the Middle Ages *Trip* meant not a journey but a resting place where journeys could be broken, and so this Trip means the way soldiers would stop for ale and kidneys beneath the castle with sunlight streaking beeches above the stableyard, a pause where swallows rested above men playing skittles down a long strip of lawn where Richard the Lionheart left once for war and a holy land he imagined and lost.

Today, *Ye Olde Trip* means an ancient public house carved into cliffs of sandstone and fern and small trees latched on to any hold they can find on the sheer cliff-edge of the world as spring returns to England slowly. It means a pub beneath a castle where in a niche in the stone walls the *cursed galleon* rests. The *cursed galleon* is a small model of a sailing ship heavy with years of dust and grime, all the wear of history and age and repetition, a toy ship left uncleaned for so long because, the story goes, quick death alighted on anyone who dared wash it of its past.

And so while I eat, I imagine the ridiculous, untimely deaths I might bring down upon myself if I were brave enough to clean the galleon of its history. I start with cholera easy as unwashed lettuce, but on I travel and run into the abutment of bridges and drown quickly as a kitten in an over-turned boat, tumble down stairs narrow as the question mark my neck turns into on landing and hemorrhage into my hands from a fall across a rake with the fire-laced riot of autumn spread around me—and all the while, in a corner above the bottles' crenellations, television from America displays a photo of a boy in a hood like a wanted poster, dark shadows on his face like heavy dust of the past, and the news anchor reports how he was chased through the deepwood of a subdivision and killed by a man convinced he was sheriff in his own private neighborhood of fear.

If *Ye Olde Trip* means history articulated in the way roads here are named for Maid Marian and Friar Tuck, it also means we remember the elegance of Sherwood where sunlight filigrees gothic tangles of limbs in a canopy of generous outlaws and ignore the major oak strung with lanterns of hung men. It means we believe the Lionheart walking out from the mist of myth to establish order, rather than the real, French-speaking Richard, who stripped and flogged those who came unasked to his coronation, people who dared go where they were not welcome until fires touched inside the lowest of clouds above their homes and blood left their bodies to paint the thatch and shoddy glamour of this kingdom.

This boy, perhaps, hoped he was free of the past when he walked home through that subdivision beneath the streetlights pooling white across the asphalt, but I should know better. It is easy for me. This morbid imaginarium of my possible deaths was all in fun, but I never thought once, thinking back on it now, that I might be torn down by a lion-heart of a man with nothing to fear but a boy in a hood with a handful of Skittles inside the small dark ship of a Florida night.

for Trayvon

V. EL CAFÉ A LA ESQUINA DE AGUA Y VIDA, SEVILLE

At the café at the corner of Water and Life
in the plaza of blood oranges at the bend
of the whitewash and archways of old stone,
between the congregation of traffic and
the soft hammers of the cathedral bells,
near baths made by Peter the Cruel and
alongside the tiny carapaces of smartcars
hived in the old Jewish quarter where
the exhausted piss-whiff of the city
wanders off into the *Jardines de Murillo*
where fists of palms and geometric rigmarole
circle the fountain—ficus and terra cotta frescoes
of the Christian everlasting: the gold leaf,
the halo, Madonna adoring—near the dead-end
of the road of death, beneath keyhole arches
at the mark of midyear and in the shadow
of *el Real Alcázar* (layered cathedral of all
that's holy here—Christian on Muslim
on Roman on something far older), where
wings of the canopy angle out to hide me
from the wallop of the noonday sun in the square
where I'm sipping a *vinho verde* that tastes
of the effervescence of granite and hot grass,
the woman at the public fountain, with an ache
and a fine delicacy, runs damp hands through
her spray of dark hair, sops the hot arch

of her neck, and trails fingers down her bare
arms the way Christ might have washed
Magdelane had he been a just bit more human.

VII. WITH FLOWERS

ou est elle la mort? toujours future ou passée?

My son and I stood beneath the sign,
Arrêté—C'est ici L'Empire de la mort,
and, then beneath massive lions and

the swirl of traffic about Montparnasse,
like Dante and a thirteen-year-old Virgil,
we dropped down into hell. The story

began slowly—starting with the technique
of excavation itself, how this city beneath
the city was constructed, tunnels emptied

and stone raised from dark quarries
in the fields to assemble the city of light above—
and built to cemeteries emptied in the old town

and all the bones carted here: six million
bones in the long tunnels beneath Paris,
bones piled like city walls topped with

crenellations of skulls, long fencing of bone
after bone, bones and the green felt of moss
gentling the faces of these citizens.

But in a monument
to comrades lost beneath a cave-in
like a sudden folding of hands after

a day of long labor, tunnel workers carved
a façade of the *Quartier de Cazerne*
into an alcove of one shaft, a classic portico

and the scalloped archways of their home
like the castle of the poets Dante found
in hell—seven gates and beyond a meadow,

fresh and green. Back in the world above,
at *Au Bouquet*, Julian and I ate a late meal
in the February sunlight that tunneled

through the cloud-cover: *vin rouge* and
chocolate chaud, charcuterie and cheese
like the rough fruit of the earth itself,

as trees rooted up into that flint-
colored sky and traffic hummed past
on the Boulevard Saint-Jacques.

IX. THE ARAB BATHS IN RONDA

If you have not seen the day of Revolution in a small town where all know all . . .
and always have known all, you have seen nothing.
—HEMINGWAY

Although once through the precise retina of stars
sunlight slipped into the arched ceiling in the steam room

where men sat and chin-wagged and watched slaves
fan steam from juniper fires through four pairs

of horseshoe porticoes below brick barrel vaults,
they really aren't Arab. All this is Roman,

a style lost in the fall of one empire and returned
in the conquest of Iberia, part of the understrata we walk on

because the world is old and full of stories,
the way towns here are named *de la Frontera*

because they were—frontier between north and south,
Roman and barbarian, then Arab and Christian,

and then Fascist and Republican, each side carrying
the small particulars of half an empire in a collection

of haversacks. Away at home, in Belfast, my son is fighting
in the school we've sent him to, with all the easy cruelty

and conviction of youth and the rain comes down
without its usual mercy as he steps from our flat

in his uniform each morning—tie and suit coat
where a red Welsh dragon squirms

like a thin and tangled river on the breast.
He carries America with him, my son,

and his small town back home like a sack
across his back that no longer protects him

from the rain or the ache of being thirteen
in a country of new syllables and old enemies,

and so I have had to tell him that the town
he left hasn't forgotten the small spring flower of his life

and moved on into its own deep summer,
but that, of course, is a lie. We lose the world

we leave behind when we cross that bridge,
like the one built atop the old aqueduct that collapsed

into the Guadalevín's thin trickle years ago,
and where, in 1936, Republican farmers

chucked 500 fascists into the gorge below
as a young man named Ernest watched and worked

it into story. It's Easter holiday and we walk
the old city's plazas of oranges and white-wash

and the bells after a lunch of oxtail, *queso y jamón ibérico,*
and a bottle of tempranillo like the nectar of smoke

and sweaty leather, down to the gate where sunlight breaks
the brick ceiling of cloud. We descend down the cobbled lane

below walls built up century by stone by century in hope
of stopping an army, each soldier arriving with

a small bundle of fire and a knife. We walk down the path
leading onward atop broken frontiers and constellations

of flagstone to the baths that aren't Arab and a past that isn't,
down to *Arroyo de las Culebras* where the slither of the river

disappears into the canyon—long shaft of willow
and bulwark of stone and stone and shadow

that divides the city, old from new,
rain sealing it all together in the end.

X. SLEEPING THROUGH IT

When the tree came down
across the fence in the night
and blustered its barky limbs
across the small lawn
and missed our bedroom
by inches, I heard only
the mute swan of my own sleep.
When I was asked to attend
the convening of the committee
on safety's evanescence,
I was hard at work adjusting
the machinery of silence.
When traffic spun past weaving
its dangerous cloth of taillights
and the light on the corner
flashed its amber Morse,
I listened to the unending
echoes of rocks in the canyon
of quiet. When the fires
of July erupted and the night
smelled of burned rubber
and oil, I was carefully
unaware of the tiny openings
of the stars. When jackdaws
belted their minor key lament,

like a low smoky chuff
in the dark, when
planes blinked across
an upturned bowl called
the sky, when happiness
and sorrow demanded
my attention,
I was memorizing
the language of hush.
When the muster of names
was shouted out and
my presence was required,
I slept on at the mercy
of the flowers in the apple
orchard as they blossomed
into moths made of white
like the ash of bodies burned on
ghats along the holy river of night.

ELEGY WITH PENELOPE &
A VINEYARD IN IT

I need to rewrite a story. I need to unweave
the whole war, raise up the burning tower,

shuttle heroes back across the sea through the warp
of the waves. I must pull the wind back

into its gold sack.
     To tell it all, I need to bring up Dionysus,
god of the smashed grape, unraveler, my friend in the night

as the suitors grumble & fuss & ride each other in their sleep,
legs thrown about like logs.
       I need to tell you how it began:

§

in a short slant of sunlight on a table in the kitchen
a man works his poems in the slow arithmetic of days

rotating towards winter, in a room above life accumulating
in the rooms below, below him, below me,

as the suitors gather like goats & the harvest assembles
in the woven silos to feed them all as the fire smudges

itself out in the afternoon before it is built again for the evening
meal—in all this it began. I arrived at Ajax

in a courtyard laid out across the enormous carpet
of his shadow & those walls the soldiers writhe

over, fires sparking in the temples like woven stars
I cannot wait to unravel. Earth all around tamped down

by the ruckus of feet, earth tamped down like brown
sugar tamped down, flame stroking the spoon.

In the sweep of my weaving I arrived
at Ajax and could go no further,

§

and here's the other half of the story: Dionysus tilts out
from inside the olives trees & offers a farmer something new,

something the world has been waiting for without knowing it.

He augers holes in a dried riverbed, plants vines wiry
as old men. He blesses the earth with a spray of piss.

Dionysus dances his little ox-foot dance & he hoes some weeds.
The farmer watches with one-eye on his daughter,

one eye on the shaggy androgyny rambling through his fields
as the vineyard thickens into old men gripping each others' shoulders &

the grapes gather in the crush. They break & juice
like small burst suns. Not long after, this man with his poems,

§

this Larry Levis, reads to a small crowd in an abandoned dormitory.

His baggy jacket & Ned Flanders mustache, the upturned
chin & slouch at the podium as he bends into the page.

Floor lighting paints a colossal shadow on the wall behind him.
He offers his poems like glasses of wine, deep swallows

of crimson, in each poem the moment held perpetually
aloft like those same glasses before they touch,

which is the image of our trust in one another,

which is the way Dionysus & the farmer get drunk together:
dust, olives & the long light of the setting sun,

the two of them around the fire. They tip the small hearts
of the wine pouches to their mouths & drain them. Then

the farmer's daughter arrives & wonders just what her dad
is up to now. They get *her* drunk & no one has any idea

what that means yet, just as no one knows I am now dismantling

the scene of Ajax's madness in the garden, unthreading
the slaughtering of the sheep as the suitors sleep on

in the hush of the great hall. The three of them clatter beneath the stars
	& bang through the orchard

wearing cooling jars as hats—slaves bark their fear into the night—
all of them drunk & stumbling. Now

§

Larry Levis is shaking my hand & the hand
of everyone in the dormitory with all its empty rooms

sleeping overhead. He is saying something kind

& elemental;
			I want to say more about this moment,
but there is nothing more to say as I slipped out from the line

& let the next one hear something kind & elemental, imperfect
as words are imperfect, as the threads of this story

spill in imperfect piles at my feet.

No one said anything about the farmer & his daughter,
no one said anything about the goat that was eating the leaves

of the vines as we opened the doors & wandered into the broad quiet
of a Midwestern night. The farmer will skin the goat that dared

to eat his vines with a long knife.
He will open the animal & let the entrails spool around his feet.

He will wear its moist pelt, dance the first tragedy with his goat feet
& as he does something vast begins.

He dances his feet into hooves & his head into horns.

He dances his pride & his age, the small field of white
he's cultivating at his temples. He dances his life &

he dances his death that is arriving without a sound in the flexing
    leaves.
He dances & the dance *around* the goat becomes the dance *of* the
    goats,

& slowly what was the goat began to be replaced by what was not
    the goat;
thus the poem is made from what is not poetic, the song

from what is not worth singing. Now he stalks past the Blue Note,
a little drunk, the crowd spreading into the broad quiet of a
Midwestern night.

Now he smells the vinegar & lines up the needle
as Ajax in his shame lines up his sword to dive on it.

I am just now banishing that moment from the fabric.

§

The farmer takes his ox cart & trundles around, showing off his vines,
pouring wine skins dark as hearts for shepherds

who drink & feel for the first time fuzzy around the eyes,
tongues sloshing in their mouths. They have been waiting

for this looseness, this easy laughter around the fire.
They have been waiting without knowing it,

which is a kind of waiting, but they don't know that either. So
when the moment comes they bring to it suspicion, the lightest of
      emotions, &

an anger which weighs them down. In the image of rumor, of how
      we cannot, finally, trust each other, all the shepherds take a turn
      dividing him:

one with a rock, one with a sickle, one with an axe, one with a hoe.

They circle him, & their ululations ring off the clouds
as their arms drop out of the dark above the fire,

his dance becomes their dance, his blood
becomes their wine.

§

It's his body the daughter finds in a trench below
the orchard after Dionysus has punted off to other fields.

It's his body she climbs as she rungs up into the tree

made of grief where she'll be found in the morning swinging
back & forth, back & forth between the axis

of what is meant and what is said,

between the two hearts that keep beating inside the body of this
story—the soft iambic of pulsing blood that becomes

a thread of wine spooling on the floor.

I would place Ajax, back in his health, standing colossal
before all the Trojan spearmen, his shadow thrown against

the great wall but now all the threads are tangled;

now he is reading from "Caravaggio: Swirl and Vortex,"
now he is planting vines.

I can stack the past like bottles of green glass chalked
with small white numerals,

I can unweave myth & fact back into the cabinets
where they are stored, packed like spools,

but something remains in the threads
even as they run down around my feet.

THE ROLLING STONES VISIT THE CAVE OF HERCULES, 1967, MOROCCO

The Stones arrived, the guidebook says, amid
drug busts and the band starting to split,
at this cave where Hercules rested

after separating Africa from Europe, shoving
the gates of Gibraltar apart and watching
the stunned flood of whales pass between

his legs, this cave where Berbers for years
worked millstones from the walls for grinding
olives and left unfinished discs stamped

in the basalt, grooved like gold records hung
in offices across London. When the band
washed up in Tangier with *kif* and hash

and the silver moons of necklaces they wore,
they trundled through streets busy with the smell
of bread baked in *ferranes* up to the Kasbah

and the Café HaHa with the sound of jajouka
in the middle distance (smatter and bash
of the cymbals and hand drums and goat pipes

tooling up) in a city where the streets narrow to arms
against the sky and the phantasmagoria of the souks.
In this cave Hercules was becoming something

that the world had never seen—half-man, half-god
who would live forever in the afterlife of the stars—
but now he was tired. He had schlepped

his way through the zodiac of his labors
and thought he was nearly done (only a garden
at the end of the world remained, with a sky

that needed to be held aloft) and there was nothing
left for him, he thought, just a chamber
carved out of rock where he could bundle

the skin of his lion and finally lay down his head,
just as Mick and the boys recline by the pool,
out of the sun, waiting for the labor

they don't know is coming—the banquet
and the quagmire of their four legendary albums,
the harrowing of the streets, the sticky, brown-

sugar, death-in-the-eyes quartet that ends
in the perfect blue garden of *Exile on Main Street*—
and smoking a hookah as Brian Jones falls apart

and Keith absconds with Anita like Pan seducing
the moon. The gift of music was given away
in this cave by a half-man, half-goat who was perhaps

only a boy wrapped in a goat's skin who stumbled
out from the edge of the darkness and began his dance
as the flutes and guitars and the swiveling drums

all started talking at the same time like Keith and Brian
playing for the last time together on "Midnight Rambler,"
that whomp of the blues harp and Keith's guitar knocking

the backbeat. The boys walk through the Kasbah
with the smell of that bread floating ahead of them
like fame as the song of the muezzin ripples out

beyond the city, arabesques ringing the open green door
of the mosque, the door that resembles the mouth
of a cave where discs are cut and grooved and

the world is only a distant melody of strife
to a workman who sleeps, his hat down across
his eyes, and waits for the afternoon's labor to begin.

RAIN, OR A LOCAL POET LONG GONE RETURNS HOME

The lightning bangs and the rain takes its cue
and looses its sacks of stones across my spring-
cleared roof, but I hear another night in another city
when rain rushed down as never before—a night
in Belfast when poets read into the rising atrium
of the Ulster Museum and rain was shrapnel
on a steel roof, rain was horses in a galloping dark,
the audience marooned there in that tower of art
and history—soaring pterodactyl crossing space
above our heads, Irish wolfhound hugely in the corner,
posters acknowledging the Troubles down the hall—
as the main lights vanished and the fingers
of emergency lighting pointed out faces in the crowd
while heavy shoulders of thunder kept us trapped
in that bamboo garden of rain that fell and fell
all around us and the rain kept coming and coming
and water flowed feet deep down Botanic
and flooded cars all along that street of bookshop
and pub, the chip shop's lights like a ship lost at sea,
until there was nothing to do but retire to the pub
across the street beneath a rain that fell like
tenacity and the weight of history that lives on
and filled Friar's Bush graveyard across from the pub—
stone-bound acre of tall grass and headstones thin
as roofing slates where the fake 'Friar's Stone' found
inside and inscribed *AD 485* is, in fact, Victorian affection

for a gothic past of mist and myth, because back then
everyone was trying to forget the bodies dead
from cholera and famine in 1847 when the island
was wet with death and the thin arms of the starving
beneath another rain that gathered like an accumulation
of syntax and the long layering of grammar
and history and hatred and dogged abandonment,
and people either left or died, which is the condensed history
of this island, and the easy answer, and wrong, because
someone had to stay behind, someone had to write it
all down, someone had to catalogue this space
made empty by rain: green land of stone and rill
and the vandalized sheep, small back room of an island
now dark and filled with chatter and pints,
a peat fire burning ancient, heaped accumulations,
and these bodies warming, ridding themselves of the rain.

for Marianne Boruch

SMACK DANIEL'S BAND PLAYS REGGAE AT THE COLLE AMENO, PONTECCHIO MARCONI, ITALY

As Chad drops the beat on a trash can and Vonn kicks cats out of the shadows with the sound of his bass, we're drinking prosecco in the heat out on the deck of the *osteria* built among the ruins of an old villa where the Germans, trying to hold on to the last tatters of the Gothic line in 1944, separated the men who couldn't work from the boys who could and filled a grave with them.

Grasshoppers in the poppies buzz like speaker feedback as the band muscles into "I Shot the Sherriff." Vonn squawks, *If I am guilty I will pay,* as Scott tosses wah-wahs into the corners of a chapel long since converted to other lives: communal houses and laundry turned semaphore on lines where it's long dry.

Beyond the gate old walls fall in on themselves in an elegant wreckage that becomes something else here beneath the sun thudding on this deck, the renovated world that wants desperately to construct something from the past's bucket of wrack and girder.

Now there are plates of hard goat cheese like a sharp and wonderful chalk, salamis fat and greased, and an apricot-colored pinot grigio like the ripe fruit of sunlight and stone. Now there is dancing and the make-shift band stumbles through the intro of "War," stops, starts again and then finds their way through the song as if following a trail made long ago up a hillside of green timber and dry grass.

It's always this way. Happiness I mean. The day's heat is strong and fresh, the wine tastes of jasmine and history, we believe, lies a long way away.

for John and Chad

FOR THE BLIND MAN IN THE *BASILICA DI SANTA CROCE*, FLORENCE.

Our stories can only carry us so far. I know
there are layers beneath the layers and
you haven't asked but I would describe
a fresco not even finished in the workshop,
discovered beneath damaged plaster here
in the *Scuola del Cuoio*. A simple Madonna
and child marked off with a draftsman's
patience, a sketch of faces each etched
with a different kind of cross. Evidence
of a man working out art's proportions
like a map in the sand: golden mean
in the plaster and articulation balanced
between the bridge in the distance
for scale and the sketched-in step-child
abandoned almost in the foreground,
clutching at the mother's skirts—all
the necessary work that gets covered over
in the finish, smoothed out and blessed
with plaster and color, that blinding light
cast by the angelic child, mother adoring.
I would describe it all—but that's easy
and I am not so foolish anymore. I know
you don't need me to tell you this.
You know the chittering of swallows as
they fill the courtyard of the cloister and

the weight of sunlight on cypress and stone.
If meaning is made of anything you will
have heard it in the sound of great space
that flows down the stairs of the Pazzi chapel,
in the rattle of the tourist dragging
his bag on the pavers as he moves toward
enormous doors flung open into the heat.

NOTES

The italicized portion of "The Country of Nostalgia" comes from the Wikipedia entry for Nostalgia, with slight modifications.

Lines in "Pineme" are borrowed from Shakespeare's Sonnet 73, *Hamlet*, and T.S. Eliot's *Four Quartets*.

"Gadreel" takes its form from an Iraqi folktale about night herons:

> *They come in the night, they do, to peck*
> *out the eyes of bad children. So be good,*
> *my child, or you'll wake up blind.*

"Dantalion" is dedicated to anyone who has ever taught a class, and more specifically to those teachers who taught us, in their last gestures, what teaching truly can mean.

"Jokes" makes use of several old jokes that were collected on *Prairie Home Companion's* Annual Joke Show.

"Forneus" is a cento made up from the *Collected Bushisms* by Jacob Weisberg.

THE HALO BRACE

Intro: Rainer Maria Rilke, "Sonnets to Orpheus."

I. "This music is the music I hear . . ." after Wallace Stevens, "Peter Quince at the Clavier.

XV. For Jennifer

XVI. "A library which was a world," retold in Jacques Derrida's "Force and Signification."

XXX. "What is your substance . . . ?" Shakespeare, Sonnet 53

XXXVIII. Jorge Luis Borges, "Tlon, Uqbar, Orbis Tertius."

XLI. For Jamie Lawrence

XLII. John 8:8

XLIII. For Jim McDermaid

XLVI. For Juliet Rodeman

XLVII. After Elizabeth Bishop

LII. For Lynne McMahon

LIII. For my parents

THE COUNTRY OF LOST SONS

Goodnight Nobody: The text is from *Goodnight Moon* by Margaret Wise Brown. This poem is dedicated to my son, Julian, and Scott Drake, whose dismembered body was found in a grass and shrub-covered lot directly across from East Ohio Street in Pittsburgh.

York Harbor: The epigraph is, of course, from "Puff the Magic Dragon," by Peter Yarrow and Lenny Lipton. © 1963, Pepamar Music.

Avenue of Chance Ascent: The members of the Basque Separatist organization specialized in attacking sites visited by Spanish tourists since 1983 after the failure of negotiations with the Spanish government to obtain the independence of the Basque province.

The Old City, Prague, 1990: In Staromestske Namesti sits the monument to Jan Hus, a church reformer burned in 1415 by the Holy Roman Emperor for heresy. "Sanctas simplicatas," can be translated, "Holy Fool." In 1969, Jan Palach, a student at Charles University, doused himself in gasoline and set himself on fire to protest the occupation of Czechoslovakia by Warsaw Pact forces.

The Night of the Barricades, Paris, 1968: On the evening of May 10, 1968, students and striking teachers organized a large march to demand freedom for five university and high-school students, jailed activists in the movement against the war in Vietnam.

Autumn and Spring: Madison, Wisconsin: Hyacinthus was a very handsome young man. Apollo fell in love with him and, in flirtatious sport, they held a contest with the discus. When Hyacinthus ran out to take up the discus that Apollo had thrown, the discus struck him down. Apollo tried to save his life, but the wound was past all cure. From Hyacinthus' blood sprung a flower—the hyacinth—and its petals carry the marks of the god's grief. As Ovid says, Apollo inscribed in its petals *ai ai legoi*, which imitates the god's suffering.

The Assassination of Luis Donaldo Colosio, 1994: Luis Donaldo Colosio was social development secretary under President Carlos Salinas de Gortari before resigning to run for Mexican president.

Fucking on the Confederate Dead: *You hear the shout*... This and several other lines have been adapted from Allen Tate's poem, "Ode to the Confederate Dead."

THE BELFAST NOTEBOOKS

Led Zeppelin Debuts "Stairway to Heaven," Ulster Hall, March 5, 1971: Belfast was blitzed by two hundred bombers of the German Luftwaffe on April 15, 1941. Apart from London, this attack represented the greatest loss of life in any night raid during the Blitz. A large number of US servicemen were stationed in Belfast at the time of the raid. Those dancing at Ulster Hall that night were not allowed to leave until the bombing ceased.

The New Faces of Belfast: The Shankill Butchers were an Ulster loyalist (Protestant) gang, led by Lenny Murphy, responsible for as many as 23 sectarian murders between 1972–79.

Certain things here are quietly American: The title is the opening line of one of the sections of Derek Walcott's book-length poem, *Midsummer*.

Stroke City: The controversy over the name of Derry/Londonderry is deep and goes back to the Plantation of Ulster, when the English brought Presbyterian Scots into northern Ireland to control the last of the autonomous Irish. My ancestors were among them.

The Mona Lisa of Belfast: The Mona Lisa of Belfast was a famous protestant mural in Lower Shankill that depicts a UFF officer pointing a rifle directly at the viewer. It was demolished on August 20th, 2015. The phrase *Quis separabit?* is the motto of, among others, the Ulster Defense Association and means *Who will separate us?*

In the Convento di San Francesco, Fiesole, Italy, on the 10th Anniversary of the Invasion of Iraq: Quotes from Canto XII of Dante's *Inferno*.

Elegy with Penelope and a Vineyard in It: Is dedicated, obviously, I hope, to Larry Levis and uses variations on several sentences from Roberto Calasso's remarkable book, *The Marriage of Cadmus and Harmony*.

ACKNOWLEDGMENTS

Over the years, I have had the pleasure of working with many different editors and publishers. I am especially grateful to those who published early versions of these poems in the following books, journals, or websites.

"Why I Write" appeared on the *AGNI* Blog, 2015.

NEW POEMS:

"Self-Portrait as Ishmael's Arm," *Beloit Poetry Journal*

"Fake News" and "Short Story for the FBI," *Blackbox Manifold*

"Country-Western Poem," *AGNI Online*

"Where do your poems come from?," *Ploughshares*

"Jokes," *Subtropics*

"Gadreel," *River Styx*

"Stop Making Sense," *Green Mountains Review*

"What are you reading?," *Sweet*

"Selected Periodic Table of the Elements (with Notes)," *Devil's Lake*

"The Country of Nostalgia" and "Telegraph Ghazal," *Drunken Boat*

"Maine Room" and "Murder Mystery Poem," *The Lark*

"What is poetry? Part 1" (as "What is the State of Poetry Today?"), *32 Poems*

"What is poetry? Part 2" and "Maine Room," *Deep Water*

"Personal," *Blue Mesa Review*

"Asbeel," *Connotation: An Online Artifact*

"This has been a test of the emergency broadcast system" and "In the Town Called Cliché," *Diode*

"Ain't Misbehavin'," "Bitches Brew," and "Lush Life," *Brilliant Corners*
"Dantalion," *Pittsburgh Post-Gazette*
"Achilles in Jasper, Texas" won the *Split This Rock* Poetry Contest, 2008

PREVIOUS COLLECTIONS:

The Halo Brace—published by and used with permission of Birch Brook Press, 1996.

The Country of Lost Sons—published by and used with permission of Parlor Press, 2004.

Renovation—published by and used with permission of Carnegie Mellon University Press, 2005.

Birdwatching in Wartime—published by and used with permission of Carnegie Mellon University Press, 2009.

"Celestial Emporium of Benevolent Knowledge"—published as a chapbook by RopeWalk Press, 2007.

"Blind Desire"—published as a limited-edition art book printed in English and Braille with companion photographs by Dennis Marsico, Dionysus Press, 2005.

The Belfast Notebooks: *Poems and Prose*—published by and used with permission of Salmon Poetry, 2017 Many of the poems also appeared in a limited-edition chapbook, *The New Faces of Belfast*, from Anchor & Plume Press, 2015.

GRATITUDE

Deep and abiding thanks are due to many people who helped the writing of this book in myriad ways, but the first thanks go to Carey Salerno—for her remarkable friendship, her ferocious belief in poetry, and her abiding love of books. To her and her wonderful staff—Alyssa and Alicia—thanks for making this book a reality.

Additional thanks go to: Christian Barter, Drew Barton, Curtis Bauer, Adrian Blevins, Ciaran Carson, Kristen Case, Anna Catone, Jerry Costanzo, Chad Davidson, Tony Deaton, Prahlad Folly, Greg Fraser, Robert Hass, Terrance Hayes, Christopher Howell, Andrew Hudgins, Rodney Jones, Cynthia Lamb, Bill Lenz, Amanda Mays, Lynne McMahon, Wes McNair, Ron Mitchell, Darren Morris, Sinéad Morrissey, Jim Murphy, Matt O'Donnell, Pat O'Donnell (no relation), Penelope Pelizzon, John Poch, Mary Jo Salter, Sherod Santos, Alan Shapiro, Luis Torres, Connie Voisine, Amy Sage Webb, Terri Witek, my parents and my sister, and to Kevin Stein—my first teacher—among many unnamed others, my students and friends, who deserve acknowledgment for their critique, their support, and their assistance in ways too many to name.

The National Endowment for the Arts, the Pennsylvania Council on the Arts, University of Missouri, Emporia State University, the Maine Arts Commission, Chatham College, the US/UK Fulbright Exchange, Queen's University Belfast, the Seamus Heaney Poetry Centre, and the University of Maine Farmington provided support during the time this book was written. My sincere *thank you* to all of them, as well.

But, as always, the highest, most-deserved gratitude is reserved for Jennifer Anne and Julian. If one of the questions this book tries to answer is "Why I Write," you are why I do everything else.

RECENT TITLES FROM ALICE JAMES BOOKS

Odes to Lithium, Shira Erlichman
Here All Night, Jill McDonough
To the Wren: Collected & New Poems, Jane Mead
Angel Bones, Ilyse Kusnetz
Monsters I Have Been, Kenji C. Liu
Soft Science, Franny Choi
Bicycle in a Ransacked City: An Elegy, Andrés Cerpa
Anaphora, Kevin Goodan
Ghost, like a Place, Iain Haley Pollock
Isako Isako, Mia Ayumi Malhotra
Of Marriage, Nicole Cooley
The English Boat, Donald Revell
We, the Almighty Fires, Anna Rose Welch
DiVida, Monica A. Hand
pray me stay eager, Ellen Doré Watson
Some Say the Lark, Jennifer Chang
Calling a Wolf a Wolf, Kaveh Akbar
We're On: A June Jordan Reader, Edited by Christoph Keller and Jan
    Heller Levi
Daylily Called It a Dangerous Moment, Alessandra Lynch
Surgical Wing, Kristin Robertson
The Blessing of Dark Water, Elizabeth Lyons
Reaper, Jill McDonough
Madwoman, Shara McCallum
Contradictions in the Design, Matthew Olzmann
House of Water, Matthew Nienow
World of Made and Unmade, Jane Mead

Alice James Books is committed to publishing books that matter. The press was founded in 1973 in Boston, Massachusetts as a cooperative, wherein authors performed the day-to-day undertakings of the press. This element remains present today, as authors who publish with the press are invited to collaborate closely in the publication process of their work. AJB remains committed to its founders' original feminist mission, while expanding upon the scope to include all voices and poets who might otherwise go unheard. In keeping with its efforts to build equity and increase inclusivity in publishing and the literary arts, AJB seeks out poets whose writing possesses the range, depth, and ability to cultivate empathy in our world and to dynamically push against silence. The press was named for Alice James, sister to William and Henry, whose extraordinary gift for writing went unrecognized during her lifetime.

Designed by Alban Fischer

Printed by McNaughton & Gunn